Marxism at the
millennium

Marxism at the millennium

Tony Cliff

BOOKMARKS

London, Chicago and Sydney

Marxism at the Millennium – Tony Cliff
First published 2000
Bookmarks Publications Ltd, c/o 1 Bloomsbury Street, London WC1B 3QE,
England
Bookmarks, PO Box 16085, Chicago, Illinois 60616, USA
Bookmarks, PO Box A338, Sydney South, NSW 2000, Australia
Copyright © Bookmarks Publications Ltd

ISBN 1 898876 66 5 (Paperback)

Printed by Larkham Printing and Publishing
Cover by Roger Huddle

Bookmarks Publications Ltd is linked to an international grouping of socialist organisations:
- **Australia:** International Socialists, PO Box A338, Sydney South
- **Austria:** Linkswende, Postfach 87, 1108 Wien
- **Britain:** Socialist Workers Party, PO Box 82, London E3 3LH
- **Canada:** International Socialists, PO Box 339, Station E, Toronto, Ontario M6H 4E3
- **Cyprus:** Ergatiki Demokratia, PO Box 7280, Nicosia
- **Denmark:** Internationale Socialister, PO Box 5113, 8100 Aarhus C
- **Germany:** Linksruck, Postfach 304 183, 20359 Hamburg
- **Greece:** Socialistiko Ergatiko Komma, c/o Workers Solidarity, PO Box 8161, Athens 100 10
- **Holland:** Internationale Socialisten, PO Box 92052, 1090AA Amsterdam
- **Ireland:** Socialist Workers Party, PO Box 1648, Dublin 8
- **New Zealand:** Socialist Workers Organization, PO Box 13-685, Auckland
- **Norway:** Internasjonale Socialisterr, Postboks 9226 Grønland, 0134 Oslo
- **Poland:** Solidarność Socjalistyczna, PO Box 12, 01-900 Warszawa 118
- **Spain:** Socialismo Internacional, Apartado 563, 08080 Barcelona
- **United States:** International Socialist Organization, PO Box 16085, Chicago, Illinois 60616
- **Zimbabwe:** International Socialist Organisation, PO Box 6758, Harare

Contents

About the author

Tony Cliff was born in Palestine in 1917, the year of the Russian Revolution. In the 1930s he became a revolutionary socialist and a follower of Leon Trotsky. After working to build a small revolutionary group in Palestine, he came to Britain after the Second World War. He broke from orthodox Trotskyism after undertaking an extensive study of the Soviet Union's Eastern European satellites.

He founded the Socialist Review Group, which became the International Socialists in the 1960s and the Socialist Workers Party in the 1970s. He wrote many books including a three volume biography of Lenin and a four volume biography of Trotsky. He died in April 2000 shortly before the publication of his autobiography, *A World to Win: Life of a Revolutionary*.

These essays were written in the last year of his life for revolutionary socialist organisations in Germany and Turkey. They are published here for the first time in English. The publishers would like to thank Cliff's comrade, companion and wife Chanie Rosenberg for her invaluable help in putting the collection together.

Chapter 1

Is Marxism still relevant?

At school we learn history as a story of great men: kings, generals, emperors. I remember learning about Cleopatra having a bath in milk. The teacher never told us who produced the milk and how many Egyptian children suffered from malnutrition for lack of milk. We were told about Napoleon going to Russia in 1812. We were not told how many Russian peasants or French peasants in uniform died as a result.

The *Communist Manifesto* makes it clear that what is significant is the action of the millions:

> The history of all hitherto existing society is the history of class struggles. Freeman and slave, patrician and plebeian, lord and serf, guild-master and journeyman, in a word, oppressor and oppressed, stood in constant opposition to one another, carried on an uninterrupted, now hidden, now open fight, a fight that each time ended, either in a revolutionary reconstitution of society at large, or in the common ruin of the contending classes.

Both Stalinist 'socialism' and social democratic 'socialism' is socialism from above. With the Stalinists this is obvious. When Stalin sneezed, every party member had to take out their handkerchief.

Social democratic 'socialism' looks, on the face of it, democratic, but in reality is completely elitist. The man and woman in the street are expected to vote in parliamentary elections once in five or four years, but leave the rest to others. If a person votes ten times in his life, he spends, let us say, 30 minutes in a democratic exercise. Abe Lincoln said, 'You can't have a society half free and half slave.' The social democratic leaders expect the mass of the people to live a lifetime in slavery and 30 minutes in democracy.

The contradictions in capitalism

Under capitalism those who work don't own the means of production and those who own the means of production don't work. Under capitalism production is social. Workers work in big units—factories, railways, hospitals—encompassing numbers of workers. Production is social, but ownership is not. The ownership is in the hands of individuals, capitalist corporations or states.

In every individual unit of production there is planning. But there is no plan to coordinate the different units of capital. In Volkswagen they produce one engine per car, one body per car, four wheels (or an additional one in reserve) per car; there is co-ordination between the different aspects of production. But there is no co-ordination between the production of Volkswagen and that of General Motors. Planning and anarchy are two sides of the same coin under capitalism.

It is useful to juxtapose capitalism to feudalism that preceded it and to socialism that will follow it.

Under feudalism there was individual production and individual ownership. Under socialism there will be social production and social ownership.

Under feudalism you cannot speak of any planning, either in an individual unit or in the economy as a whole. Under socialism planning will apply to every unit of the economy and to the economy as a whole.

Because of the massive dynamics and productivity of capitalism at the same time as anarchy exists, we face the phenomenon of poverty in the midst of plenty. For thousands of years people starved because there was not enough food. Capitalism is the only system of society in which people starve because there is too much food. In the United States they build special boats to carry grain in which they are able to open the bottom and sink the grain to keep up its price.

Poverty and wealth take extreme forms as never before in history. It was calculated that 58 multi-billionaires have wealth equal to the income of half of humanity. This half of humanity includes not only the poor but also the relatively affluent.

Competition between capitals and exploitation of workers

Under feudalism the feudal lord exploited and oppressed the serfs as a means of making the feudal lord's life better. As Marx put it, 'The walls of the stomach of the feudal lord is the limitation of the exploitation of the serfs.' What motivates Ford to exploit his workers is not his interest in consumption. If that were the case, the burden of the capitalists would be small. Ford employs 250,000 workers internationally. If every worker gave £1 a day in the form of surplus value, it would be ample for the Ford owners to live on. Not only this. Because the dynamism of the economy is much greater than the dynamism of anyone's consumption, the burden on the workers would have declined over time. But the motive of exploitation is not the consumption of the capitalist, but capital accumulation. To survive in the competition with General Motors, Ford has to retool the factories again and again to invest more and more capital. The other side of the anarchy of competition between the capitalists is the tyranny under which workers are suffering in every capitalist unit.

The nature of the capitalist state

Everywhere we are told that the state rises above society, that the state represents the nation. The *Communist Manifesto* makes it clear that the state is a weapon of the ruling class:

> The executive of the modern state is but a committee for managing the common affairs of the whole bourgeoisie.

Elsewhere Marx writes that the state is 'armed bodies of men and their accessories'—army, police, courts and prisons.

Marx also called the army the 'slaughter industry', and it is dependent on real industry. The productive forces determine the destructive forces. In medieval times, when the peasant had a horse and a wooden plough, the knight had a horse (a better one) and a wooden sword. In the First World War, when millions were mobilised into the army, other millions were mobilised into industry to produce the guns, bullets, etc. Today, when a finger can press a button and thus transfer thousands of pounds abroad, a finger on another button can annihilate 60,000 in Hiroshima. The slaughter industry and industry fit like a glove on the hand. If a Martian found a glove he would not understand why there are five fingers, but if he knew the glove was to cover a hand with five fingers, it would be obvious. Also the social structure of the army reflects the social structure of society. If the army has generals, colonels going down to privates, it is similar in the factory where there is manager, foreman, worker. One hierarchy fits the other hierarchy.

The proletarian revolution

To expropriate the capitalists the working class must take political power. But, Marx argued, the workers cannot simply take the existing state machine, because the present state mirrors the hierarchical structure of capitalism. The workers have to smash this hierarchical state machine, and replace it with a state in which there is no standing army, no permanent bureaucracy, all officials are elected and can be removed, and no representative earns more than the workers they represent. Marx came to this conclusion after watching the Paris Commune of 1871, in which the workers achieved just this. The *Communist Manifesto* says:

> All previous historical movements were movements of minorities, or in the interest of minorities. The proletarian movement is the self-conscious, independent movement of the immense majority, in the interest of the immense majority.

Marx explained why we need a revolution: the ruling class won't give up wealth and power unless forced; and the working class won't get rid of 'the muck of centuries' without a revolution.

Capitalism both unites workers and divides them. Competing for jobs, housing and so on, splinters the working class; fighting the bosses unites the workers. The maximum unity and the heart of the revolution is the mass strike. The revolution is not a one-night affair, but a process of strikes, demonstrations and so on, culminating in the workers physically taking power.

Violence, so often misrepresented as the revolution itself, is, as Marx said, 'the midwife of a new society'. Note: it is the 'midwife', not the baby itself—just a help.

The most important aspect of the revolution is the spiritual changes of the working class. To give an example. Under Tsarism Jews were harshly persecuted. There were pogroms against Jews. They were not allowed to live in the two capitals, Petrograd and Moscow, without special permission, and there were a host of other major restrictions. Comes the revolution: the chairman of Petrograd Soviet was a Jew, Trotsky; the chairman of Moscow Soviet a Jew, Kamenev; the chairman of the Soviet Republic a Jew, Sverdlov; the head of the Red Army a Jew, Trotsky.

Another demonstration of the huge spiritual changes. During 1917, during the month of the revolution, Lunacharsky held meetings of

30,000 to 40,000 people and would speak for two to three hours on subjects like William Shakespeare, Greek drama, etc.

The conditions for revolution, Lenin explained, are four:

(1) the general deep crisis of society;

(2) the working class makes it clear it cannot stand going on as at present;

(3) the ruling class loses confidence that it can continue to rule as up to now and they therefore split and quarrel, and

(4) the existence of a revolutionary party.

Socialism or fascism

In the above quote from the *Communist Manifesto* Marx wrote that the class struggle 'ended, either in a revolutionary reconstitution of society at large, or in the common ruin of the contending classes'. He came to this conclusion based on the experience of the decline of Roman slave society. Spartacus was defeated, the slaves did not manage to overthrow the slave-owning class, society declined, the slaves disappeared and were replaced by serfs, and the slave-owners by feudal lords. (The invasion of the German tribes was only one element in this process.)

Engels formulated the same idea by speaking about the alternatives facing humanity as socialism or barbarism. Rosa Luxemburg developed it further. Neither knew as much about barbarism as we do. Engels died in 1895; Rosa Luxemburg was murdered in January 1919. Both did not know about the gas chambers, about Hiroshima and Nagasaki, about the mass famine in Africa, etc.

When the Nazis were knocking at the gates of power, the leaders of the German Social Democratic Party (SPD) thought the alternative to Nazism was the status quo. They therefore voted for Field Marshal Hindenburg to be president, because he was a conservative, not a Nazi. (On 30 January 1933 he called on Hitler to become the prime minister of Germany.) The Social Democrats supported Brüening's Emergency Decrees that cut workers' conditions, demoralised them and helped the Nazis along. Fritz Tarnow, the 'theoretician' of the trade unions, stated, 'Capitalism is sick. We are the doctors of capitalism.' Marx said the working class was the gravedigger of capitalism. There is a difference between a doctor and a gravedigger. The doctor will put the pillow underneath the sick man's head; the gravedigger will put it over his head.

Because fascism is a movement of despair, while socialism is a movement of hope, to fight fascism it is necessary not only to fight the fascists but also the conditions that lead to despair. One has to fight the rats, but also the sewers in which the rats multiply. One has to fight the fascists, but also capitalism that creates the conditions that breed fascism—unemployment, bad housing, social deprivation, etc.

More relevant than ever

The contradictions of capitalism today are much deeper than they were when Marx died in 1883, contradictions that appear in deep mass slumps, wars that go on and on in one country after another, etc. The working class is much stronger today than in 1883. As a matter of fact the working class of South Korea is larger than the total working class of the world when Marx died. And South Korea is only the eleventh economy in the world. Add to them the American, Japanese, Russian, German, British workers, etc, and the potential for socialism is greater than ever.

Chapter 2

Why do we need a revolutionary party?

Uneven consciousness in the working class

Why do we need a revolutionary party? The basic reason is in two statements Marx made. He stated that 'the emancipation of the working class is the act of the working class' and at the same time he said that 'the prevailing ideas of every society are the ideas of the ruling class.'

There is a contradiction between these two statements. But the contradiction is not in Marx's head. It exists in reality. If only one of the statements was correct, there would not be a need for a revolutionary party. If the emancipation of the working class is the act of the working class, and that is all, then, to be honest, we need do nothing about fighting for socialism—let's sit with folded arms and smile. The workers will emancipate themselves!

If, on the other hand, 'the prevailing ideas of every society are the ideas of the ruling class', and that is all, workers will always accept the ideas of the rulers. Then we can sit with folded arms and cry because nothing can be done.

The reality is that the two statements are correct. The class struggle always expresses itself, not just in a conflict between workers and capitalists, but inside the working class itself. On the picket line it is not true that workers are there to try and prevent the capitalist from working. The capitalists never worked in their lives so they will not work during a strike. What the picket line is about is one group of workers trying to prevent another group of workers from crossing the picket line in the interests of the employers.

The question of workers' power, what Marx called the dictatorship of the proletariat. Why would you need a dictatorship of the proletariat if the whole working class is united and there are only a tiny minority of capitalists in opposition? You could say go home, and we'd finish with the bosses. If the whole working class is united we could spit at them and flood them into the Atlantic!

The reality is that there will be workers on one side and backward workers on the other side. Because 'the prevailing ideas of every society are the ideas of the ruling class', the workers are split between different levels of consciousness.

Not only this. The same worker can have split consciousness in his head. He or she can be a good wages militant, can hate the boss, but when it comes to black people it's a different story.

I remember we lived with a chap, a printer, in the same house, a very skilled man. He was going on holiday and I asked, 'Are you flying tomorrow?' He said, 'No, I can't fly tomorrow. It's Friday the 13th. We'll have to wait till Saturday.' This man in the 20th century has some ideas from 1,000 years ago.

Against opportunism and against sectarianism

You can stand on a picket line and next to you is a worker who makes racist comments. You can do one of three things. You can say, 'I'm not standing with him on a picket line. I'm going home because there no one makes racist comments.' That is sectarianism because if 'the emancipation of the working class is the act of the working class' I have to stand with him on a picket line.

The other possibility is simply avoiding the question. Someone makes a racist comment and you pretend you haven't heard and you say, 'The weather is quite nice today!' That's opportunism.

The third position is that you argue with this person against racism, against the prevailing ideas of the ruling class. You argue and argue. If you convince him, excellent. But if you don't, still when the scab lorry comes you link arms to stop the scabs because 'the emancipation of the working class is the act of the working class.'

The revolutionary party: university of the working class

The bourgeoisie didn't have a revolutionary party 20 years before their revolution. The Jacobins in France didn't exist before 1789.

Why do we have to start 20, 30 or 50 years before the revolution? We have to start to talk about the need for a revolutionary party to lead the working class in struggle, in revolution.

The Jacobins were established during the act of the revolution itself. Why? Because when you look to the relations between the capitalists and the nobility, it is different from the relationship between the capitalists and the working class.

It is true that the capitalists had to overthrow the nobility and the working class has to overthrow the capitalists, but there is a big difference. It is not true the nobility owned all the wealth and the capitalists were paupers. The capitalists were rich even before the revolution. They could turn around to the nobility and say, 'All right, you own the land; we own money, we own the banks. When you go bankrupt how do you save yourself? You mix your blue blood with my gold, you try to marry my daughter.' When it came to ideas they could say, 'All right, you have priests, we have professors. You have the Bible—we have the Encyclopaedia. Come on, move over.'

The capitalists were independent intellectually from the ideas of the nobility. They influenced the nobility much more than the other way around.

The French Revolution started with a meeting of les États généraux (the Three Estates)–the nobility, the priesthood and the middle classes. When it came to the vote it was the nobility and the priesthood who voted with the capitalists, not the other way around.

Is our position similar? Of course not. We cannot turn to the capitalists and say, 'All right, you own Ford, General Motors, ICI, we own a pair of shoes.' In terms of ideas I don't know how many capitalists are influenced by *Socialist Worker*. Millions of workers are influenced by the *Sun*!

The revolutionary party of the bourgeoisie could appear during the very act of the revolution. They didn't have to prepare; they were confident. What happened on 14 July 1789? Robespierre, leader of the Jacobins, suggested they build a statue to Louis XVI on the site of the Bastille. He didn't know that three years on he'd cut off the head of Louis XVI. Where does the name Jacobins come from? It came from the monastery where they met. If they had known that four years later they were going to expropriate the church lands they wouldn't have named themselves after a monastery.

They were independent, they were strong and they could deal with the issues. We have a completely different situation. We belong to an oppressed class that lacks the experience of running society, because capitalists don't only own the material means of production but the mental means of production. Because of that we need a party—the party is the university of the working class. What Sandhurst is to the British Army, the revolutionary party is to the working class.

Marx says in the *Communist Manifesto* that communists generalise from the historical and international experience of the working class. In other words, you don't learn from just what you experience. My own experience is tiny. Any one of us has fantastically little experience. You need to generalise and to do that you need an organisation that does it. I can't myself know about the Paris Commune. I wasn't there. I was very young in 1871! So you have to have someone who gives you the information.

Trotsky therefore wrote that the revolutionary party is the memory of the working class.

Three types of workers' parties

There are three types of workers' parties: revolutionary, reformist and centrist.

The *Communist Manifesto* described the nature of the revolutionary party in these words:

'The communists are distinguished from the other working class parties by this only: (1) In the national struggles of the proletarians of the different countries, they point out and bring to the front the common interests of the entire proletariat, independently of all nationality. (2) In the various stages of development which the struggle of the working class against the bourgeoisie has to pass through, they always and everywhere represent the interests of the movement as a whole.

The communists, therefore, are, on the one hand, practically, the most advanced and resolute section of the working class parties of every country, that section which pushes forward all others; on the other hand, theoretically, they have over the great mass of the proletariat the advantage of clearly understanding the line of march, the conditions, and the ultimate general results of the proletarian movement.

The second type of workers' parties are the reformist parties. In a speech to the Second Congress of the Communist International in 1920 Lenin defined the Labour Party as a 'capitalist workers' party'.

He called it capitalist because the politics of the Labour Party do not break with capitalism. Why did he call it a workers' party? It is not because the workers voted for it. At that time more workers voted for the Conservative Party; and the Conservative Party is of course a capitalist party. Lenin called the Labour Party a workers' party because it expressed the urge of workers to defend themselves against capitalism. When one watches the Labour Party conference on television, it is clear that the members of the Labour Party express different urges than the Tory party. At the Tory party conference the applause comes when speakers attack trade unionists and blacks, and praise the army, police, etc. In the Labour Party conference the applause comes when a speaker declares the need for a better health service, better education, housing, etc.

Between the revolutionary parties and reformist parties there is a third kind of party, the centrist parties. Their main characteristic is fudge. They are neither one nor the other. The vacillate between the two. A horse produces horses, a donkey donkeys. When a horse and a donkey mate they produce a mule. A mule does not produce anything; it is sterile. With a revolutionary party there is historical continuity. It can go up or down, but it continues. With a reformist party there is historical continuity. But not with the centrists. In 1936 the POUM party in Spain had 40,000 members. Now the POUM is dead as a dodo. The Independent Labour Party in Britain had four MPs from the 1945 general election. Now there is not even a remnant of the ILP. A similar story attaches to the SAP in Germany, which was a mixture of people who came from the right, Blandlerite, wing of the KPD (German Communist Party), pacifist elements of the SPD and others from a mixed bag. It was quite a large party in the early 1930s. Now there is no sign of it.

A revolutionary teaches and learns from the working class

The revolutionary party has to lead the working class based on all the experience of the past. OK, so the party teaches the workers, but then arises the simple question: 'Who teaches the teacher?' It is extremely important to understand that we can be taught by the working class. All the great ideas come from the workers themselves.

If you read Marx's *Communist Manifesto* he speaks about the need for a workers' government, the dictatorship of the proletariat. Then in 1871 he writes that the workers cannot take hold of the old state machine: they have to smash it—the old standing army, the bureaucracy, the police. We have to smash all this hierarchical structure and establish a new kind of state—a state without a standing army or a bureaucracy, where every official is elected, where every official gets the same rate of pay as the average worker. Did he find this out because he worked so hard in the British Museum? No, no. What happened was that the workers of Paris had taken power and that's exactly what they did.

Marx learnt from them. The Stalinists always claim that Lenin invented the idea of the soviet. Of course in the Stalinist literature Lenin invented everything! They had a concept of religious hierarchy. We have the correspondence of Lenin, and when workers established the first soviet in Petrograd in 1905, Lenin wrote four days later—what the hell is that for?

In the struggle the workers needed a new form of organisation. They learnt the hard way that if they had a strike committee in one factory it was not effective in a time of revolution. You need a strike committee which covers all the factories. And that's what the soviet was: delegates from all the factories meeting together to run the show. They did it. Lenin followed them. The party has always to learn from the class, always.

Is the party always in advance of the class? The answer is that by and large the revolutionary party is in advance of the class. Otherwise it is not a revolutionary party. So when it came to 1914 and the outbreak of the First World War, the Bolsheviks were far in advance of the class. The Bolsheviks were against the war while the majority of the workers supported it.

Then comes 1917. In 1917 you find Lenin says again and again in August and September that the party is lagging behind the class, the class is more advanced than the party and we have to run quickly to catch up with the class. The reason is a simple one. For such a long time the workers had lacked confidence so they were behind the revolutionary party. Comes a change in the situation and they change very, very speedily.

The problem with revolutionaries is that we need a routine to survive. But the routine enters into you. You take it for granted that you are in advance of the working class. But when the workers start moving you find you are so bloody backward! The revolutionary party has to catch up with the working class. The party is not just a group of people. They are the revolutionaries and from now on they are always leading. That's rubbish. You have to fight and fight to lead all the time. You have to learn all the time, to advance all the time.

This is not just in time of revolution. You will find in the workplace that someone can be in the SWP for 20 years, a good comrade, and there's someone completely new, who joined a few months ago, and when it comes to activity the new comrade is far more advanced than the comrade who joined 20 years ago. You find this again and again.

You don't win the leadership like you have money in the bank. If you have money in the bank it gains interest. A revolutionary leadership is nothing like this. You have to win the leadership every day, every month. So for revolutionaries what counts is what they did last week, what they're doing this week and what they're doing next week. You can learn from all the experience of 100 years but the important thing is what you're doing this week. You have to fight for leadership.

Members of the reformist parties are passive and accommodating

Because the reformist party wants to get the maximum vote, it looks to the lowest common denominator. It adapts itself to the prevailing ideas.

Do you really believe that none of the Labour MPs know about the oppression of gays and lesbians? But still during the elections of 1987 Patricia Hewitt, Neil Kinnock's secretary, leaked to the *Sun* (of all papers) an attack on the 'loony left' in the councils which support gays and lesbians. Why did she do it? Because she thought that was the way to become popular. I have a leaflet from a man called John Strachey. He called himself a Marxist. In the 1929 election he stood for parliament and he had a problem—he looked Jewish. So he issued a leaflet with the heading 'John Strachey is British' and challenged anyone who said he was Jewish to go to court. Why did he say it? I have to say I'm a Jew, but if any member of the SWP is called a Jew they'd say, 'Of course I'm a Jew. I'm proud of it.' You don't deny it.

But if you want the maximum numbers you have to adapt to the prevailing ideas. The reformist parties are therefore large parties but extremely passive. For example, there is a book called *Labour's*

Grassroots where the age composition is given. In 1984 there were 573 branches of the Labour Party Young Socialists, in 1990 only 15. There were three times more members aged 66 and above than aged 25 and below. Labour Party members were asked how much time they devoted to Labour activities in the month: 50 percent said none, 30 percent said up to five hours a month, an hour a week, and only 10 percent said between five and ten hours.

Extreme passivity—that is the nature of the Labour Party. The other side of the same coin is bureaucratic control. The bureaucrats dominate the party.

Then there is the sect. Its members say quite simply, 'We want to march only with people who agree with us. We care only about people who agree with us.'

The revolutionaries are those who are separate from the majority of the working class but at the same time are part of the working class. The question for revolutionaries is how to relate to non-revolutionary workers. How you relate to people who agree with you 60 percent and how, through the struggle, you can move that to 80 percent. If you are a sectarian you say, 'You don't agree with me on 40 percent, I don't care about you.' If you are a revolutionary you say, 'We agree on 60 percent, let's start with that and I'll argue with you about the 40 percent that we don't agree and in the struggle try to convince you.'

Democratic centralism

What about the structure of the revolutionary party? Why do we speak about democratic centralism?

Let us first understand why we need democracy. If you want to go from London to Birmingham you need a bus and a driver. You don't need democratic discussion because we've done it before so we need one good driver and one good bus. The problem is that the transition from capitalism to socialism is something we've never experienced before. We don't know.

If you don't know, there's only one way to learn—by being rooted in the class and learning from the class. It is not simply that on everything democracy solves the problem. If you want to know if there's a decline in the rate of profit, if Marx is right, don't put it to the vote! It doesn't mean anything. Either he's right or he's wrong. Think about it, read about it and decide.

There are things you must put to the vote. Everything that is connected to our struggle must be put to the test. Because we simply don't know. Because if 'the emancipation of the working class is the act of the working class' the working class through their own experiences will teach us.

There is a beautiful description Lenin gives of when he was in hiding after the July Days in 1917 when the Bolshevik Party became illegal and its press was smashed. The Bolsheviks were accused of being German agents. Lenin did not know how far the power of reaction had been consolidated. He describes eating with a worker he was hiding with and the worker gave him bread and said, 'The bread is good. They, the capitalist class, are frightened of us.' Lenin says:

> The moment I heard him I understood about the class relation of forces. I understood what workers really think—that the capitalists are still frightened of us, although we are illegal, although we are beaten. Still it is not a victory of counter-revolution.

If you want to know if the workers are confident how do you know? You can't have a ballot in the press, they don't give you the opportunity. You can't meet every individual.

You cannot make a working class revolution without a deep democracy. And what the revolution is about is raising the working class to become the ruling class, about creating the most democratic system in history. Unlike under capitalism where every five years you elect someone to misrepresent you, here it is a completely different story. Under capitalism you elect the MPs but not the employers. Under capitalism we don't vote on whether to close a factory. We don't elect the army officers or the judges. In a workers' government everything is under workers' control. Everything is in workers' power. It is the most extreme form of democracy.

So if all this is true, why do we need centralism?

First, the experience is uneven, workers have different experiences, you have to collect that experience together. Even in the revolutionary party the members are influenced by different pressures. They are influenced by the general picture and by the section of the workers to which they belong.

To overcome this sectionalism, this narrow experience, you need to centralise all the experience and division. Again you need the centralism because the ruling class is highly centralised. If you are not symmetrical to your enemy you can never win.

I was never a pacifist. If someone uses a stick on me I have to have a bigger stick! I don't believe a quotation from Marx's *Capital* will stop a mad dog attacking me. We have to be symmetrical to our enemies. That is why I cannot understand the anarchists when they come and say they don't need a state. The capitalists have a state. How do you smash a state without an opposition state?

Anarchists always deny the state. When they had enough strength they joined the government. That's what they did in Spain during the civil war when they joined the government. Why? Because there is no good denying something unless you smash it and if you smash it you have to replace it. What do you have to replace it with? Armed bodies of workers. And that's what the workers' state is.

The need for a mass revolutionary party

When we speak of the party leading the class it is not just a question of experience, knowledge and roots. The leadership must use the language of workers, have the spirit of workers. You have to relate to them because that's what leadership is about. You talk and listen, you don't only talk. You talk in language they understand.

But that's not enough. We need a big party. To lead the working class you need a mass party. The SWP is the smallest mass party in the world. It is a tiny party. The Bolshevik Party in 1914 had 4,000 members. After the February 1917 revolution they had 23,000 members. In August 1917 they had a quarter of a million. With a quarter of a million you can lead an industrial working class of three million.

The German Communist Party in 1918 had 4,000 members. Even if they were all geniuses they could not have won the revolution. You need a sizeable party because in order to lead you need to have a base in every factory.

I mentioned the July Days. When Lenin was accused of being a German spy 10,000 workers out of 30,000 at the Putilov factory struck for the day saying they trusted Lenin. Why? Because they had 500 Bolsheviks in Putilov factory.

If you want to lead millions you need hundreds of thousands in the party. Even the ANL Carnival, 150,000-strong, a marvellous achievement, in terms of the revolution was still a small thing. Even for this, we needed six, seven or eight thousand SWP members to organise it.

I detest it when people think Marxism is some sort of intellectual exercise: we interpret things, we understand, we are more clever. Marxism is about action and for action you need size. For action you need power. We need a mass party—of half a million.

Chapter 3

The importance of Marxist theory

Again and again Lenin repeated that there cannot be a revolutionary party without revolutionary theory. Marxism is defined by Marx and Engels as scientific socialism. Science, whether physics, chemistry or Marxism, cannot be learnt by rote as a collection of slogans. It has to be studied seriously.

When Marx and Engels write that revolutionaries have to generalise the historical and international experience of the working class movement, this cannot be done except through study, through theory. One cannot know about the Paris Commune from one's own experience. For that one has to read the books. Trotsky formulated the same idea in different words when he said the revolutionary party was the memory of the class, and the university of the class. At a university students study theory.

One has to learn the past in order to prepare for the future. Karl Radek, a leading Bolshevik, described in his memoirs of Lenin how in the middle of the stormy days of 1917 Lenin told him he should read a book on the French Revolution, as it would help him understand the tasks ahead. During this same period Lenin wrote one of his most important theoretical works, *State and Revolution*. St Just, at the time of the French Revolution, said, 'Those who make half a revolution dig their own graves.'

All revolutions start as half revolutions. The new co-exists with the old. Thus the February 1917 revolution got rid of the Tsar, got rid of the police, established the soviets, workers' committees in the factories—all this was new. But the old survived: the generals remained in the army, the capitalists continued to own the factories, the landlords the land, and the imperialist war continued.

When Lenin returned to Russia in April 1917, 10,000 workers and soldiers welcomed him at the Finland Station in Petrograd. The chairman of the Petrograd Soviet, the right wing Menshevik Chkheidze, greeted him with a big bouquet of flowers, and declared, 'In the name of the victorious Russian Revolution you are welcomed.' Lenin pushed the bouquet aside, turned to the thousands of workers and soldiers and said, 'What victorious Russian Revolution? We got rid of the Tsar! The French got rid of their king in 1792. The capitalists still own the factories, the landlords own the land, the imperialist war goes on. Down with the Provisional Government! Down with the war! Land, bread and peace! All power to the soviets!' One historian, Sukhanov, described the scene. One would have thought the thousands of workers and soldiers would have shouted, 'Hoorah!' to Lenin. But they were completely dumbfounded. They were so excited by the end of Tsarism, the end of the police, that they could not understand why anyone should criticise the set-up. The only voice heard in the silence was that of Goldenberg, an ex-member of the Central Committee of the Bolshevik Party. He shouted, 'Lenin is mad! He's completely mad!' Because Lenin understood the words of St Just very well, he went on to lead the revolution to its final victory.

Since 1917 there have been many revolutions that went only halfway and therefore ended with a counter-revolution.

To give a few examples. In November 1918 the revolution in Germany got rid of the Kaiser and established workers' councils, soviets, in Germany. Alas, the generals remained, the factory owners remained. In 1919 army officers murdered Rosa Luxemburg, Karl Liebknecht and other Communists. And many years later the Nazis came to power in Germany.

In 1979 mass strikes culminated in a general strike led by workers' councils (*shoras*) and overthrew the Shah of Iran. The leadership of the workers were the Communist Party (Tudeh) and the Fedayeen, both followers of Moscow. They argued for unity of the Iranian people and all Muslims. They compromised with Ayatollah Khomeini and he repaid them with a massacre.

The third example is Indonesia. In the early 1960s the Indonesian Communist Party had 3 million members, far more than the Bolsheviks had in 1917 (quarter of a million). There were also 10 million in organisations associated with the Indonesian Communist Party. But the leadership, being Stalinist, argued for the unity of the Indonesian nation and all Muslims. They supported the bourgeois nationalist president of Indonesia, Sukarno. In 1966 a subordinate of General Sukarno, General Suharto, made a coup which led to the massacre of between a 500,000 and 1 million Communists.

We have to learn from the past to prepare for the future. We have to study Marxist economics so that we understand the contradictions in the capitalist system, the forces that lead to explosions in it.

To lead is to foresee. In order to foresee one must have a clear theoretical understanding of the economy, society, politics, history, philosophy.

It is not good enough for a minority of party members to know the theory. Everybody should know it. Lenin wrote that in a revolutionary party there is no rank and file, therefore everybody must have a knowledge of Marxism. The revolutionary party is not a copy of a capitalist factory or the capitalist army. In the factory the managers decide and the workers have to obey. In the capitalist army the officers command and the soldiers stand to attention. In a revolutionary party every member has the power of thinking, deciding and acting.

Of course in practice there is unevenness in the level of consciousness and of knowledge of theory inside a revolutionary organisation. But this unevenness has to be levelled up. The worst damage that can be done inside a revolutionary party is if there is an attack on the intellectuals inside the party, in the name of a proletarian attitude. As a matter of fact such an attack is not so much on the intellectuals but on the workers in the party. It is an insult to the workers as it assumes the workers are unable to grasp theory. Why do you think Marx spent 26 years of his life writing *Das Kapital?* As a matter of fact he never finished the book. Only Volume 1 was published in his lifetime. Volumes 2 and 3 were edited by Engels after Marx's death. Why do you think the Marxists in Russia organised evening classes for workers in the 1890s, teaching them Marxism?

One of the best books in defence of the role of the intellectuals in a revolutionary party is Lenin's *What is to be Done?* written in 1902. His opponents, whom he called economists, thought workers were unable to go beyond trade union consciousness, beyond the demand for money or a shorter working week.

Again, it was the Italian revolutionary Marxist Gramsci who wrote about the need to create worker intellectuals.

It was the right wing in the German Social Democratic Party who attacked Rosa Luxemburg: she was too intellectual for them. Probably they didn't like the fact that she was non-German (being Polish) and a woman. Similarly in 1923 when Lenin was on his deathbed Stalin attacked Trotsky as an intellectual, and later condemned him as 'cosmopolitan', that is, hinting that he was a Jew.

Underestimating the significance of theory in a revolutionary party is basically an insult to workers, assuming they are unable to grasp ideas and are uninterested in them.

Reading Marxist literature and listening to Marxist lectures is not enough to make members of a revolutionary party grasp Marxist theory. One must have a close periphery to the party members. When Lenin says everyone in a revolutionary party is a leader it means every member must give a lead to workers outside the party. If, say, a member of the SWP relates to a couple of people in his workplace, neighbourhood or school he's in, these people will pose questions he will have to answer.

To give one example, one might say, 'You call for revolution, but look, the Russian Revolution led to tyranny. Why should we support revolution?' If the party member can explain what happened to Russia after the revolution, like the defeat of the German Revolution that led to the isolation of Russia, that led to the degeneration of the regime, to the rise of Stalin who became the gravedigger of the revolution and the builder of state capitalism, then the party member has a clear grasp of the theory. The dialogue with non-party people will make clear to him what he knows, and more important, what he does not know and should learn.

The heart of Marxism is dialectics, the dialogue between members and non-members. How can the individual party members get people arguing with them? The key is selling the revolutionary paper, not only on demonstrations or in the streets, but in the routine of selling to a few individuals in the workplace, the neighbourhood or school, so that the seller knows the individuals and has discussions with them over time.

Lenin wrote that the revolutionary paper is the organiser of the party. How does it organise? Not only internally, by organising the selling of the paper and collecting money for it, but also by getting the members to organise the periphery. In the SWP we take it for granted that besides the sale on demonstrations, in the streets or at mass meetings, the routine sale of individual party members to their periphery is of the greatest significance. An organisation that has no significant periphery is not a revolutionary organisation but a passive sect that is bound to wither away. 'Revolutionaries' without a periphery are like fish out of water.

Chapter 4

'Globalisation'—myths and realities

In recent years a new shibboleth has entered into the vocabulary—
globalisation. Leaders of all political parties, whether conservative
or reformist, accept this term as God-given. The same applies to the
press, television, company reports, union leaders. In a nutshell it boils
down to the statement that the world market and the multinationals are so powerful that the workers in every country, or in any part
of the multinational, are completely powerless. And so also is the
national state.

Edward Mortimer, writing in the *Financial Times*, a right wing conservative paper, cited the *Communist Manifesto* to support the theory
of globalisation. He quoted the following words from the *Communist
Manifesto*:

> The need for a constantly expanding market chases the bourgeoisie over
> the whole surface of the globe. It must nestle everywhere, settle every-
> where, establish connections everywhere.
>
> The bourgeoisie has through its exploitation of the world market
> given a cosmopolitan character to production and consumption in
> every country. All old established national industries have been de-
> stroyed or daily are being destroyed. They are dislodged by new in-
> dustries...that no longer work up indigenous raw materials, but raw
> materials drawn from the remotest zones, industries whose products are
> consumed not at home, but in every quarter in the globe... In place of
> the old local and national seclusion we have intercourse in every di-
> rection, universal interdependence of nations.

Edward Mortimer, in claiming that Marx was the progenitor of
the theory of globalisation, intended to pay him homage, but actually it is an insult. I shall make a few comments comparing Marxist
economics with bourgeois economics.

Marx made it clear that he owed a great intellectual debt to the
classical economist Adam Smith, and even more to David Ricardo.

But he also made it clear that his theory was not simply a continuation of classical economic theory, but also its breaking, its negation. The subtitle of Marx's *Capital* is *A Critique of Political Economy*.

Adam Smith, in his *Wealth of Nations* (published in 1772), describes very well the impact of the division of labour. He describes a pin-making factory in which each worker does a different repetitive job. This division of labour increases productivity. Marx accepted this but added that the division of labour makes the worker half-human. In this is rooted his concept of alienation. There is a round hole fitting a round peg; there is a square hole fitting a square peg. Alas, there is not a hole in the image of a human being. Workers, therefore, are not simply shaped by the system. They are not clay being modelled by big objective factors, but active subjects who resent the pressure from outside, and fight it.

For Adam Smith and Ricardo the search for profit is a natural activity. For Marx it is historically conditioned. The market, the competition between different capitalists, or at present capitalist companies, or capitalist countries, forces each of them to accumulate capital. If they fail they are doomed. The anarchy of capitalism, the competition between units of capital and the tyranny in each capitalist enterprise are two sides of the same coin. The capitalists fighting one another impose the cost of the fight on the workers, and the workers react by fighting back. They are not simply the objects of history. They are the subjects of history. The theory of globalisation pushes the idea of power at the top and powerlessness at the bottom of society to its extremes.

The globalisation theory thinks this is justified. It is part of the free market ideology.

When immigrants try to get into a country, especially if they have the wrong skin colour, they are simply economic migrants, to be condemned. When Volkswagen decided to spend over £430 million on buying Rolls Royce from Britain, that's alright. If the employer imposes a speed-up, that's alright. If the workers resist it, that's criminal sabotage. The movement of capital is not motivated by economics. Again, the radio gives news items like: 'Good news; ICI profits rose last year by 20 percent.' A few minutes later: 'Bad news; workers are greedy; they are demanding a 5 percent wage rise.'

The power of workers in the multinationals

On the face of it, it is obvious that the workers in one factory that is part of a multinational company are powerless. If a quarter of a million workers are employed by Ford, how can a factory of a few thousand in Britain stand up to Ford management?

But the reality is the very opposite. When 3,000 General Motors brake parts workers went on strike in Dayton, Ohio, in 1996, they shut down General Motors operations across the United States, Canada and Mexico. Over 125,000 General Motors workers were laid off within days. The strike cost the company around $45 million a day, and the Clinton government screamed at both sides to settle.

When an almost general strike took place in Denmark, Saab was forced to stop car production in Sweden because it ran out of essential components from Danish suppliers. The assembly of Saab's convertible motors in Finland was also forced to stop. Volvo also announced that its production lines in Sweden and the Netherlands had been very badly affected.

In 1988, when Ford workers in Britain struck, they brought the whole of Ford Europe to a halt within three or four days.

Because of the multinationals, the impact of an individual group of workers can be much greater than ever before. One need only compare the above examples with the first general strike in history that took place in England in 1832. Then workers had to move from one factory to another to 'turn over' the workers.

Behind the theory of globalisation there is complete mechanical formal logic. The dialectic is completely foreign to it. The logic of the globalisation theory is similar to that which motivated the Pentagon when it launched its war on Vietnam. They were convinced that the United States military machine was omnipotent and that the Vietnamese were relatively powerless. And the argument went like this. In the 19th century Britain beat India into submission. The military machine of the United States in the 1960s was incomparably stronger than the military machine of Britain in the 19th century. At the same time Vietnam is a much smaller country with a much smaller population than India. If Britain could win in the 19th century, the United States could certainly have a walkover in the 20th century.

Looked at dialectically the picture is exactly the opposite. In the Indian uprising of 1857, when a British soldier was killed, how much damage did it do to Britain? How much is a British soldier, a worker in uniform, worth? Let us say £100. The American military machine is incomparably greater. A US aeroplane is worth, let us say, $1 million. What a temptation for a Vietnamese to throw a hand grenade at it.

Globalisation and the national state

Another argument of the proponents of the globalisation theory is that now the national state can do nothing about the level of employment, that globalisation killed Keynesianism.

From the beginning of the Second World War until 1973 the world witnessed the longest economic boom in the history of capitalism. This was attributed by the prevailing orthodoxy at the time to Keynesianism. The policy of cutting taxation, keeping interest rates low, increasing state expenditure, managing demand so that the economy could expand—this was what Keynesianism was all about. Probably the most enthusiastic expression of support for Keynesianism was in Anthony Crosland's book, *The Future of Socialism*, published in 1956. According to Crosland the anarchy of capitalism was withering away and with it class conflict. The system was becoming more and more rational and democratic. Capitalism itself would peacefully dissolve. All the talk about production being dedicated to making profit rather than meeting human need, was, according to Crosland, sheer nonsense. 'Private industry is at last becoming humanised.'

A 'peaceful revolution' had begun in which class conflict would be unthinkable: 'One cannot imagine today a deliberate offensive alliance between government and employers against the unions,' wrote Crosland. 'We stand in Britain on the threshold of mass abundance.' Socialists should divert their attention away from economic issues. To what?

> ...we shall turn our attention increasingly to other, and in the long run more important, spheres - of personal freedom, happiness, and excitement... more open-air cafes, brighter and gayer streets at night, better and more hospitable hoteliers and restaurateurs... more murals and pictures in public places, better designs for furniture and pottery and women's clothes, statues in the centre of new housing estates, better designed street lamps and telephone kiosks, and so on ad infinitum.

The description of capitalism in its old age as being humane and rational looked to me at the time preposterous, and now even more so. Capitalism that was, to use Marx's words, born 'covered in blood and mud', could not change qualitatively. As a matter of fact the barbarity of capitalism today is much worse than it was 100 years ago. Think about the gas chambers, about Hiroshima and Nagasaki, about the estimated 20 million children dying in the Third World every year because the banks are squeezing those countries dry.

Unemployment, which reached 8 million in Germany in 1933, disappeared a couple of years later, not because Hitler read Keynes, but because of the rearmament programme. The explanation of the long boom was given by the theory of the permanent arms economy. In March 1957, in an article called 'Perspectives for the Permanent War Economy', I tried to explain the impact of rearmament on the stability of capitalism, and how also the contradictions in this process were bound to undermine the boom. In a nutshell I explained that if all the key capitalist countries spent significant resources on armaments it would open markets, and slow the decline of the rate of profit. But if a couple of important players did not participate, and spent much less on armaments, they would benefit from the boom more than those that did, and they would have more resources to spend on modernising their industries, instead of spending them on tanks and aeroplanes. And these countries would win in the competition. And this is exactly what happened. While the United States, Russia and Britain spent massively on defence, West Germany and Japan spent peanuts. The mark and the yen became far stronger relative to the dollar and the pound. In 1973, following the Vietnam War, the dollar collapsed, the price of oil pushed through the roof, and Keynesianism was declared dead.

At the 1976 Labour Party conference, the Labour prime minister, James Callaghan, declared:

> We used to think you could spend your way out of a recession, and increase employment by cutting taxes and boosting government spending. I tell you in all candour that that option no longer exists...

Keynesianism gave way to monetarism. Thatcher's policies took shape before she was elected, for, in the words of Peter Riddell, political editor of the *Financial Times*, 'If there has been a Thatcher experiment, it was launched by Denis Healey (the Labour Chancellor of the Exchequer).'

In the face of the storm, reformism is completely bankrupt. It is like having an umbrella made of paper. It is quite useful so long as there is no rain.

To challenge the attack of capitalism, to defend reforms, one must go beyond reformism. Only revolutionaries can fight at present consistently for reforms.

If the capitalist decides to close the factory, workers have to challenge his right of ownership. If to solve unemployment the working week has to be cut radically, without loss of pay, and the capitalist says it does not pay him to keep the factory open, workers have again to challenge his ownership of the factory.

Between capitalism and socialism there is an abyss—you cannot, as the reformists believe, move from one system to the other gradually. One cannot cross an abyss by a number of small steps. If anyone is in doubt about this, you can put it to the test. Find a tall building in your town, go to the top, look into the distance for another tall building. If you can cross from the one to the other by a number of small steps, reformism has proved its viability.

Chapter 5

The Stalinist regime—state capitalism

Autopsy

Nine years ago the Berlin Wall collapsed. Shortly afterwards the Stalinist regimes in Eastern Europe and Russia followed suit.

Fifty-one years ago, in 1947, I came to the conclusion that the Stalinist regime was state capitalist. I wrote a couple of books to develop the theory. But of course one cannot be sure of one's own ideas unless the test of events confirms them. The collapse of the Stalinist regime made it possible to confirm or refute the theory. If one doctor tells a patient he has cancer and another that he has tuberculosis, when a post-mortem is carried out after his death one can find out who was right.

The collapse of the Stalinist regime makes such a post-mortem possible. If Russia was a socialist country or the Stalinist regime was a workers' state, even though a degenerated or deformed one, the collapse of Stalinism would have meant that a counter-revolution had taken place. Of course workers would have defended a workers' state in the same way that workers always defend their unions, however right wing and bureaucratic they may be, against those who try to eliminate the union. Workers know from their own experience that the union, however feeble, is a defence organisation of workers. Workers in a unionised workplace earn higher wages and have better conditions than if there are no unions.

Did the workers in Russia and Eastern Europe defend the regime in 1989-91 Of course not. There workers were completely passive. There was less violence at the time than during the miners' strike in Britain in 1984-85. The only country where the regime was defended, and violently, was Romania. But there it was not defended by workers, but by the Securitate, the secret police.

Secondly, if there was a counter-revolution, the people at the top of society would have been removed. But characteristic to the collapse of the Stalinist regime was that the same personnel, the nomenklatura, who had managed the economy, society and politics under Stalinism, continued to be at the top. The years 1989-91 were not a step backward or a step forward for the people at the top, but simply a step sideways.

Therefore, it is clear that there was not a qualitative change between the Stalinist regime and what exists at present in Russia and Eastern Europe. As at present no one denies that the regime is capitalist—ergo, it was capitalist before.

The birth of state capitalism in Russia

The October Revolution of 1917 brought the working class to power in Russia. The impact of the revolution internationally was absolutely massive. Workers' revolutions took place in Germany, Austria, Hungary, and mass Communist parties rose in France, Italy and elsewhere. Lenin and Trotsky were absolutely convinced that the fate of the Russian Revolution depended on the victory of the German Revolution. Without it, they repeated again and again, we are doomed.

Tragically, the German Revolution (1918-23) ended in defeat. The lack of a revolutionary party with experienced cadres doomed the revolution. Again and again we see proletarian revolutions that did not end in victory for lack of a revolutionary party: Spain and France 1936; Italy and France 1944-45; Hungary 1956; France 1968; Portugal 1974; Iran 1979; Poland 1980-81.

The defeat of the German Revolution in 1923 led to a swing towards pessimism and right wing adaptation in Russia. Stalin campaigned openly against Trotsky in 1923. He was aided by the fact that Lenin was on his deathbed and out of circulation for about a year. Trotsky's explanation of the rise of Stalinism as the product of the isolation of the Russian Revolution and pressure of world capitalism was absolutely correct. Hence his description at that time of the Stalinist regime as a degenerated workers' state was apt.

However, what happens if the pressure of world capitalism goes on and on. Will the quantity of the pressure change its quality?

If a mad dog attacks me I need to be symmetrical to it. If it uses violence I have to use violence. Of course my teeth are not equal to his, so I have to use a stick. If I kill the mad dog, the symmetry ends. If the mad dog kills me the symmetry likewise ends. But what happens if I am not strong enough to kill the mad dog, he isn't strong enough to kill me, and we are trapped in the same room for months on end? Nobody will know the difference between the mad dog and me.

The Soviet regime was attacked by the armed forces of Germany, Britain, the United States, France, Italy, Japan, Romania, Finland, Latvia, Lithuania, Turkey. These armies, together with the White Russian armies did not manage to beat the Red Army. On the other hand, the revolutionary government of Russia did not manage to beat the capitalist governments of the world. So in the end the pressure of world capitalism forced the Stalinist regime to become more and more similar to that of world capitalism. The laws of motion of the economy and of the Russian army were identical to those of world capitalism.

When in 1928 Stalin declared that within 15 or 20 years Russia would have caught up with the advanced industrial countries, it meant that in the period of one generation Russia would achieve what took Britain over 100 years of the industrial revolution. In Britain it took three centuries for the enclosures to get rid of the peasantry to facilitate the development of capitalism. In Russia the peasantry were expropriated in three years by so-called 'collectivisation'.

Tens of millions of peasant families were expropriated and forced into the collective farms to facilitate the squeezing of surplus grain out of them to be sold on the world market to buy machinery, and also to feed the millions of new industrial workers cheaply. Millions were sent into slave camps in Siberia, the gulags. The horrors of Stalin's collectivisation reminds one of Marx's description of the enclosures in *Capital* Volume I. He writes, 'Capitalism from its birth to its death is covered in blood and mud.'

Slave labour in Russia reminds one of the role of slavery in the United States in oiling the wheels of American capitalism, and also the role of the slave trade in developing capitalism in Britain: 'The walls of Bristol are covered with the blood of the negroes.'

When Stalin built his industrial-military machine he had to start from a much weaker base than the countries he faced, but with ambitions no smaller than theirs. If Nazi Germany had tanks and aeroplanes, the military machine that Stalin built could not reflect the productive forces of Russia (after all, in 1928 the peasants had no tractors but wooden ploughs, the *sokha*) but had to reflect those of Germany.

The industrialisation of Russia was very much orientated on building heavy industry as the base for the armaments industry.

One piece of research I did that I found extremely interesting was to compare the production of the different five-year plans. I found the targets of the first, second, third, fourth and fifth five-year plans and compared them. (In Russia under Stalin nobody would have dared to do this.)

When it comes to heavy industry, the target for steel for the first five-year plan was 10.4 million tons; for the second, 17 million, the third 28 million, the fourth (resulting from the war) 25.4 million, and the fifth 44.2 million. It is clear the graph is shooting steeply upwards. The same applies to electricity, coal, pig iron, etc.

When it comes to consumer goods the picture is completely different. For example, cotton goods: the first five-year plan target was 4.7 million metres; the second 5.1; third 4.9; fourth 4.7. Thus over 20 years the target did not rise at all. For woollen goods the picture is even more dismal. The first five-year plan aimed to raise production to 270 million metres; the second to 227; the third to 177; the fourth to 159. The targets cut production over 20 years by nearly 40 percent.

Russia was very successful in producing sputniks, but not in producing shoes.

Capitalism is dominated by the need for capital accumulation. Ford has to invest otherwise he will be beaten by General Motors. Competition between capitalist enterprises forces every one of them to invest more and more, to accumulate more and more capital. Competition between the capitalists also forces every one of them to increase the exploitation of the workers. The tyranny of capital over workers is the other side of the coin of competition between capitals.

The same applies to the Stalinist tyranny towards the workers and peasants of Russia. The harsh exploitation, including the gulag, was the by-product of the competition between Russian capitalism and other capitalist powers, above all Nazi Germany.

Since 1947 I have never used the words Soviet Union or USSR. Both are complete lies. There were no soviets in Stalinist Russia. In all elections there was only one candidate standing in each constituency (the same as in elections in Nazi Germany), and he never got less than 99 percent of the vote, and not more than 100 percent, except in one case. In the 1947 election to the Supreme Soviet Stalin got over 140 percent. *Pravda* the next day explained: people in neighbouring constituencies came to vote for Stalin to show their enthusiastic support. Usually the result of the voting was announced after the poll took place, except in one case: in a 1940 referendum in Latvia, Lithuania and Estonia regarding joining the USSR, TASS, the Moscow news agency, made a mistake and announced the result one day in advance of the vote. The *London Times* therefore published the results before the vote took place.

We can't call it union. Union is a voluntary association. There was no more union between Ukraine and Russia than between India and Britain. It was an empire, not a union. The third letter in USSR, the S, stands for socialist. Russia was not socialist, but state capitalist. The last letter, R, stands for republics. They were not republics, ie democracy, but totalitarian tyranny.

Arguments against the theory of state capitalism

Three main arguments are brought forward to discount the theory of state capitalism. First, capitalism is identical with private property. In Russia the means of production was state owned, not privately owned.

Secondly, capitalism is not compatible with planning. The Russian economy was a planned economy.

Thirdly, what was necessary in Stalinist Russia was to carry through a political revolution to change the government structure, and that's all, while under capitalism what is necessary is to carry through also a social, not only a political revolution.

We shall deal with each of the arguments in turn.

In 1847 Proudhon, a muddled French socialist, wrote in his book, *The Philosophy of Poverty*, that capitalism is equal to private property. Marx, in a scathing critique of Proudhon, entitled *The Poverty of Philosophy*, wrote, 'Private property is a juridical abstraction.' If private property is equal to capitalism, than under slavery we had capitalism because there was private property; under feudalism we had capitalism because there was private property. Proudhon's ideas are a mishmash. The form of property is only a form, it does not tell you the content. There can be private property with slavery, with serfdom and with wage labour. If someone says, 'I've a bottle full of stuff,' it doesn't tell you what the stuff is. It can be wine, it can be water, it can be rubbish. Because the container and the content are not the same, it means the same content can be put into different containers. The water can be put in a bottle, in a glass, in a cup. If private property can contain slavery, serfdom and wage labour, then of course slavery can be with private property and with state property. The pyramids of Egypt were built by slaves. I'm sure no slave said to another slave, 'Thank heaven we are not working for a private owner but for the Pharaoh, ie the state, that owns us.' In medieval times the dominant relations were between serfs living in villages and the feudal lord of the manor. But there was another kind of serfdom—serfs working on church property. The fact that the church was not owned by individuals did not make the burden of the serfs on church lands any lighter.

What about the second argument, that in Stalinist Russia there is a planned economy, while under capitalism there is no plan. Not correct. The characteristic of capitalism is that there is a plan in the individual unit, but no planning between units. In the Ford factory there is a plan. They will not produce one and a half engines per car, nor three wheels per car. There is central command about how many engines, wheels, etc they produce. There is a plan, but there is anarchy between Ford and General Motors. In Stalinist Russia there was a plan for the Russian economy, but there was no plan between the Russian economy, and, let us say, the German economy.

The third argument about differentiation between a political and a social revolution falls flat in a situation where the state is the repository of the wealth. In France in 1830 there was a political revolution. The monarchy was overthrown, the republic established. This did not change the social set-up because the owners of wealth were the capitalists, not the state. Where the state is the repository of wealth, to take the political power from the rulers is to take their economic power. There is no separation between political and social revolution.

Stalinism disoriented and demoralised the international working class movement

Once Stalin took complete control of the Russian government he subordinated the Communist parties everywhere to the needs of Russian foreign policy.

A few examples. On the eve of Hitler's victory in Germany, when Trotsky called for a united front of all workers' organisations to stop the Nazis, Stalin called the Social Democratic Party of Germany 'social fascists', and Trotsky also.

When, a couple of years after Hitler's victory, the right wing French prime minister, came to Moscow and signed an alliance between France and Russia, there was a new tune: Communists should support democratic France. They henceforth voted for the military budget in France, and so forth.

In August 1939, after the Hitler-Stalin pact, the Communist parties took a new turn. When Poland was occupied on the West by Nazi Germany and on the East by Russia, Molotov, foreign minister of Russia, declared, 'One blow from the East and one blow from the West and this ugly creature of the Versailles Treaty is no more.' It is true that Poland was an ugly creature. But Molotov could have added, three million Jews were no more, and millions of Poles were no more.

I shall never forget the editorial in *Pravda* on 1 May 1940, that spoke of the two peace-loving nations, the Soviet and German nations, and that was Hitler's Germany.

When in June 1941 Germany invaded Russia the line of the Stalinist parties changed radically. Again and again in *Pravda* appeared the slogan, 'The only good German is a dead German.' In 1943 I read a story in *Pravda* by Ilya Ehrenburg. He described how a German soldier, facing a Soviet soldier, put his hands up and said, 'I am the son of a blacksmith.' This was clearly a class statement. What was the reaction of the Russian soldier? Ehrenburg reports that he said, 'You are still a bloody German,' and bayonetted him.

The zigzags quite often caught local Communist Party leaders out. A couple of months after the beginning of the Second World War I was arrested, and was in the same prison as the general secretary of the Palestinian Communist Party. When the war broke out he thought that it was an anti-fascist war, as he had argued for months before. So he decided to volunteer to join the British army. But government wheels move slowly, and after two months he got a reply to his appeal, saying he could leave prison and join the army. But meanwhile he found out that the war was not an anti-fascist war, so he refused to leave prison and join the army. There were four Trotskyists in the prison, and we used to say we were prisoners, but that Meir Slonim, the general secretary, was a volunteer prisoner. As a matter of fact the zigzags in the Communist Party were demonstrated in one street of Haifa. On one wall appeared the slogan: 'Long live the anti-fascist war.

PCP [Palestinian Communist Party]'; next to it another slogan: 'Down with the imperialist war. PCP'. When Germany invaded Russia in 1941 another slogan appeared, 'Down with Hitler and his secret ally, Churchill. PCP.' Shortly afterwards another slogan appeared: 'Long live the Red Army and its ally the British army. PCP.' And all these slogans referred to one and the same war.

Towards the end of the war, when the revolutionary upheavals in Europe were massive, the Communist parties carried out the Moscow policy of dousing the fires. In August 1944 the French underground, led by the Communist Party, kicked the German army out of Paris. Maurice Thorez, general secretary of the French Communist Party, flew from Moscow and declared in Paris, 'One army, one police, one state.' And so the French underground was disarmed.

In Italy it was again the resistance movement, led by the Communist Party, that managed to break the hold of Mussolini. But Togliatti, general secretary of the Italian Communist Party, rushed from Moscow to declare support for a government of allies of the king, who had collaborated with Mussolini, and the generals, who were friends of Mussolini.

We can go on and on giving more and more examples of the betrayal of the revolution in one country after another by the Stalinist parties. The revolutionary potential at the end of the Second World War was much greater than at the end of the First. The Stalinist parties played a crucial role in preventing this potential from becoming actual.

The significance of the theory of state capitalism

For over 60 years Stalinism had massive support in the international working class movement. It pushed revolutionary socialism, Trotskyism, to the margins. The appeal of Stalinism as Communist was extremely significant.

Now, with the collapse of the Stalinist regime in Russia things have changed.

In February 1990 Eric Hobsbawm, the guru of the British Communist Party, was asked, 'In the Soviet Union, it looks as though the workers are overthrowing the workers' state.' Hobsbawm replied, 'It obviously wasn't a workers' state, nobody in the Soviet Union ever believed it was a workers' state, and the workers knew it wasn't a workers' state.' Why hadn't Hobsbawm told us this 50 years ago or even 20 years ago?

The extreme ideological disorientation of the British Communist Party is clearly demonstrated by the minutes of their Executive Committee meetings in the wake of the collapse. Nina Temple, general secretary of the party, said:

> I think the SWP was right, the Trotskyists were right that it was not socialism in Eastern Europe. And I think we should have said so long ago.

Reading Nina Temple's statement, one need but think what would have happened if the Pope declared that God does not exist. How would the Catholic church survive?

The disarray among the Stalinist parties throughout the world is overwhelming. Those of us who declared Russia to be state capitalist long before the collapse of the Stalinist regime established a bridgehead to the future, preserved the authentic tradition of Marxism, of socialism from below.

The Stalinist parties worldwide had massive support. Stalinism affected many socialists who considered themselves to be non-Stalinist or even anti-Stalinist. The Achilles heel was the wrong conception of what Stalinism really was. They considered Stalin to be the heir of the revolution, not its gravedigger. There is as much in common between Stalin and October as between the Catholic church with its wealth and the oppression of the poor and the Inquisition, on the one hand, and the carpenter of Nazareth who overturned the usurers' table and said, 'It is easier for the camel to go through the eye of a needle than for the rich man to go to paradise.'

Chapter 6

Mao, Castro, Che and the national movements

Deflected permanent revolution

(1) Three concepts of revolution
Trotsky developed his theory with the 1905 revolution in the background. Practically all Marxists of the day, from Kautsky to Plekhanov to Lenin, believed that only advanced industrial countries were ready for socialist revolution. To put it crudely, they argued that countries would achieve workers' power in strict conformity with the stage to which they had advanced technologically. Backward countries could see their future image mirrored in the advanced countries. Only after a long process of industrial development and a transition through a parliamentary bourgeois regime could the working class mature enough to pose the question of socialist revolution.

All the Russian social democrats—Mensheviks as well as Bolsheviks–postulated that Russia was approaching a bourgeois revolution, resulting from a conflict between the productive forces of capitalism on the one hand, and autocracy, landlordism, and other surviving feudal structures on the other. The Mensheviks concluded that the bourgeoisie would necessarily lead the revolution, and would take political power into their own hands. They thought that the social democrats should support the liberal bourgeoisie in the revolution, at the same time defending the special interests of the workers within the framework of capitalism by struggling for the eight-hour day and other social reforms.

Lenin and the Bolsheviks agreed that the revolution would be bourgeois in character and that its aim would not overstep the limits of a bourgeois revolution. 'The democratic revolution will not extend beyond the scope of bourgeois social-economic relationships...' wrote Lenin in 1905. Again '...this democratic revolution in Russia will not weaken but will strengthen, the domination of the bourgeoisie.' He returned to the theme again and again.

It was not until after the revolution of February 1917 that Lenin discarded this view. In September 1914, for example, he was still writing that the Russian Revolution must limit itself to three fundamental tasks: 'the establishment of a democratic republic (in which equality of rights and full freedom of self-determination would be granted to all nationalities), confiscation of the estates of the big landowners, and application of the eight-hour day.'

Where Lenin differed, fundamentally, from the Mensheviks was in his insistence on the independence of the labour movement from the liberal bourgeoisie, on the need to carry the bourgeois revolution through to victory against the resistance of the bourgeoisie.

Trotsky was as convinced as Lenin that the liberal bourgeoisie could not carry out any revolutionary task consistently, and that the agrarian revolution, a fundamental element in the bourgeois revolution, could only be carried out by an alliance of the working class and peasantry. But he disagreed with him about the possibility of an independent peasant party, arguing that the peasants were too sharply divided amongst themselves between rich and poor to be able to form a united and independent party of their own.

'All the experience of history,' he wrote '...shows that the peasantry is completely incapable of playing an independent role.' If in all revolutions since the German Reformation the peasants had supported one faction or another of the bourgeoisie, in Russia the strength of the working class and the conservatism of the bourgeoisie would force the peasantry to support the revolutionary proletariat. The revolution itself would not be confined to the carrying out of bourgeois democratic tasks, but would proceed immediately to carry out proletarian socialist measures. Trotsky wrote:

> The proletariat grows and strengthens together with the growth of capitalism. In this sense, the development of capitalism signifies the development of the proletariat toward the dictatorship.
>
> But the day and hour when power passes into the hands of the proletariat depend directly not upon the state of the productive forces, but upon the condition of the class struggle, upon the international situation, finally, upon a series of subjective factors: tradition, initiative, readiness for struggle...
>
> In an economically backward country, the proletariat can come to

power sooner than in the economically advanced countries. In 1871 it had consciously taken into its hands the management of social affairs in petty bourgeois Paris—in truth for two months—but it did not for one hour take power in the robust capitalist centres of England and the United States. The conception of some sort of automatic dependence of the proletarian dictatorship upon the technical forces and resources of the country is a prejudice derived from an extremely over-simplified 'economic' materialism. This view has nothing in common with Marxism.

The Russian Revolution, in our opinion, creates such conditions under which the power can pass over to the proletariat (and with a victorious revolution it must) even before the policy of bourgeois liberalism acquires the possibility to bring its state genius to a full unfolding.

Another important element in the theory was the international character of the coming Russian Revolution. It would begin on a national scale, but could only be completed by the victory of the revolution in the more developed countries:

How far, however, can the socialist policy of the working class go in the economic conditions of Russia? Only one thing we can say with certainty: it will run into political obstacles long before it will be shackled by the technical backwardness of the country. Without direct state support from the European proletariat the working class of Russia cannot remain in power and cannot convert its temporary rule into a prolonged socialist dictatorship.

The basic elements of Trotsky's theory can be summed up in six points:

(1) A bourgeoisie which arrives late on the scene is fundamentally different from its ancestors of a century or two earlier. It is incapable of providing a consistent, democratic, revolutionary solution to the problem posed by feudalism and imperialist oppression. It is incapable of carrying out the thorough-going destruction of feudalism, the achievement of real national independence and political democracy. It has ceased to be revolutionary, whether in the advanced or backward countries. It is an absolutely conservative force.

(2) The decisive revolutionary role falls to the proletariat even though it may be very young and small in number.

(3) Incapable of independent action, the peasantry will follow the towns—must follow the leadership of the industrial proletariat.

(4) A consistent solution of the agrarian question, of the national question, a break-up of the social and imperial fetters preventing speedy economic advance, will necessitate moving beyond the bounds of bourgeois private property. The democratic revolution grows over immediately into the socialist, and thereby becomes a permanent revolution.

(5) The completion of the socialist revolution 'within the national limits is unthinkable... Thus, the socialist revolution becomes a permanent revolution in a new and broader sense of the word; it attains completion only in the final victory of the new society on our entire planet.' It is a reactionary, narrow dread, to try and achieve 'socialism in one country.'

(6) As a result, revolution in backward countries would lead to convulsions in the advanced countries.

Mao's rise to power

The industrial working class played no role whatsoever in the victory of Mao. Even the social composition of the Chinese Communist Party was completely non working class. Mao's rise in the party coincided with its transformation from a working class party. Towards the end of 1926 at least 66 percent of the membership were workers, another 22 percent intellectuals and only 5 percent peasants. By November 1928 the percentage of workers had fallen by more than four-fifths, and an official report admitted that the party 'did not have a single healthy party nucleus among the industrial workers.' The party admitted that workers comprised only 10 percent of the membership in 1928, 3 percent in 1929, 2.5 percent in March 1930, 1.6 percent in September of the same year, and virtually nothing at the end of it. From then and until Mao's final victory the party had no industrial workers to speak of.

So unimportant were workers in Communist Party strategy during the period of Mao's rise to power that the party did not find it necessary to convene a National Congress of Trade Unions for 19 years after the one held in 1929. Nor did it bother to seek workers' support, as witnessed in its declaration that it did not intend to maintain any party organisation in the Kuomintang-controlled areas during the crucial years 1937-45. When, in December 1937, the Kuomintang government decreed the death penalty for workers who went on strike or even agitated for a strike while the war was in progress, a Communist Party spokesman told an interviewer that the party was 'fully satisfied' with that government's conduct of the war. Even after the outbreak of civil war between the Communist Party and the Kuomintang, hardly any Communist Party organisations existed in the Kuomintang areas, which included all the industrial centres in the country.

Mao's conquest of the towns revealed more than anything else the Communist Party's complete divorce from the industrial working class. Communist leaders did their best to prevent any workers' uprisings in the towns on the eve of their being taken. Before the fall of Tientsin and Peking, for example, General Lin Piao, commander of the front, issued a proclamation:

> [calling on people] to maintain order and continue in their present occupations. Kuomintang officials or police personnel or provincial, city, country or other level of government institution, district, town, village or Pao Chia personnel…are enjoined to remain at their posts…

At the time of the crossing of the Yangtze River, before the great cities of central and south China (Shanghai, Hankow, Canton) fell to them, Mao and Chu Teh again issued a proclamation:

> It is hoped that workers and employees in all trades will continue to work and that business will operate as usual… officials of the Kuomintang Central, Provincial, Municipal or County Governments of various levels, or delegates of the 'National Assembly', members of the Legislative and Control Yuans or People's Political Council members, police personnel and heads of Pao Chia organisations…are to stay at their posts, obey the orders of the People's Liberation Army and People's Government.

The working class obliged and remained inert. A report from Nanking on 22 April 1949, two days before the People's Liberation Army occupied it, described the situation in this way:

Nanking's populace is showing no signs of excitement. Curious crowds were seen this morning to gather at the river wall to watch the gun duel on the opposite side of the river. Business is going on as usual. Some shops are closed, but it is due to lack of business... Movie houses are still showing to packed houses.

A month later a *New York Times* correspondent wrote from Shanghai:

The Red troops began putting up posters in Chinese instructing the populace to be calm and assuring them they had nothing to fear.

In Canton:

After their entry the Communists made contact with the police station and instructed the officers and men to remain at their posts to keep order.

Castro's revolution

A case in which neither the working class nor the peasantry played a serious role, but where middle class intellectuals filled the whole arena of struggle, is Fidel Castro's rise to power. C Wright Mills's book *Listen Yankee*, which is a more or less authentic monologue spoken by the Cuban leaders, deals first of all with what the revolution was not:

...the revolution itself was not a fight...between wage workers and capitalists... Our revolution is not a revolution made by labour unions or wage workers in the city or by labour parties, or by anything like that ...the wage workers in the city were not conscious in any revolutionary way...

The peasantry was hardly involved in Castro's army. As late as April 1958, the total number of armed men under Castro numbered only about 180 and at the time of Batista's fall had only grown to 803.

The Castro movement was middle class. The 82 men under Castro who invaded Cuba from Mexico in December 1956 and the 12 who survived to fight in the Sierra Maestra all came from this class.

From the outset Castro's programme did not go beyond the horizon of broad liberal reforms acceptable to the middle classes. In an article to the magazine *Coronet* of February 1958, Castro declared that he had no plans for expropriating or nationalising foreign investments:

I personally have come to feel that nationalisation is, at best, a cumbersome instrument. It does not seem to make the state any stronger, yet it enfeebles private enterprise. Even more importantly, any attempt at wholesale nationalisation would obviously hamper the principal point of our economic platform—industrialisation at the fastest possible rate. For this purpose, foreign investments will always be welcome and secure here.

In May 1958 he assured his biographer, Dubois:

Never has the 26th of July Movement talked about socialising or nationalising the industries. This is simply stupid fear of our revolution. We have proclaimed from the first day that we fight for the full enforcement of the Constitution of 1940, whose norms establish guarantees, rights and obligations for all the elements that have a part in production. Composed therein is free enterprise and invested capital as well as many other economic, civic, and political rights.

As late as 2 May 1959 Castro declared to the Economic Council of the Organisation of American States in Buenos Aires:

We are not opposed to private investment... We believe in the usefulness, in the experience and in the enthusiasm of private investors... Companies with international investments will have the same guarantees and the same rights as the national firms.

The impotence of the contending social classes, workers and capitalists, peasants and landlords, the inherent historical weakness of the middle class, and the omnipotence of the new Castro elite, who were not bound by any set of coherent, organised interests, explains the ease with which Castro's moderate programme of the years 1953-58, based on private enterprise, was cast aside and replaced by a radical programme of state ownership and planning. It was not before 16 April 1961 that Castro announced that the revolution had been socialist. In the words of the president of the republic, Dr Oswaldo Dorticos Torrado, the people 'one fine day...discovered or confirmed that what they have been applauding which was good for the people was a socialist revolution.' An excellent formulation of the Bonapartist manipulation of the people as the object of history, not its conscious subject!

What went wrong with the theory?

While the conservative, cowardly nature of a late-developing bourgeoisie (Trotsky's first point) is an absolute law, the revolutionary character of the young working class, point (2), is neither absolute nor inevitable. The reasons are not difficult to appreciate. The prevailing ideology in the society of which the working class forms a part is that of the ruling class; in many cases the existence of a floating, amorphous majority of new workers with one foot in the countryside creates difficulties for autonomous proletarian organisations; lack of experience and illiteracy add to their weakness. This leads to yet another weakness: dependence on non-workers for leadership. Trade unions in the backward countries are almost always led by 'outsiders'. Thus it is reported from India:

> Practically all Indian unions are led by persons who have no background in industry, ie 'outsiders'...many of the outsiders are associated with more than one union. A national leader of considerable stature remarked that he was president of about 30 unions, but added that obviously there was nothing he could contribute to the work of any of these!

Weakness and dependence on outsiders leads to personality cults. Many unions are still in the habit of revolving around personalities. A strong personality dominates the union. He determines all its policies and actions. The union becomes known as his union. Workers look up to him to solve all their difficulties and to secure for them all their demands. They rely upon him as their defender and champion and are prepared to follow him wherever he may lead them. There is a large element of hero worship in this attitude. There is a good number of such heroes in the movement. They are of help in getting for workers some of their demands, but not much help in developing self reliant democratic organisations. The latter will not grow unless workers learn to stand on their own legs and not pathetically rely on eminent personalities to solve all their problems for them.

Another weakness of the labour movement in many backward countries is its dependence on the state. It was reported from India:

> The state has already taken upon itself many of the functions which, in a free society, normally belong to trade unions. As things stand at present the state, and not collective bargaining between employers and employees, plays the major part in the determination of wages

and other conditions of work. That was inevitable to some extent owing to the background condition of the economy and the weakness of workers and their trade unions.

And from French West Africa:

…direct union efforts against employers have rarely brought real wage increases to African labour; it is rather social legislation and the labour movement's political influence which have been responsible for most of the real wage gains of recent years.

And from Latin America:

Union representatives seek to achieve their gains through government interference and dictation.

The most important factor determining whether the working class in the backward countries is actually revolutionary or not is a subjective one, namely, the activities of the parties, particularly the Communist parties, that influence it. The counter-revolutionary role of Stalinism in backward countries has been dealt with too often to need repetition here.

A concatenation of national and international circumstances makes it imperative for the productive forces to break the fetters of feudalism and imperialism. Peasant rebellions take on a deeper, broader sweep than ever before. In them is rooted also national rebellion against the economic ruin brought by imperialism and for the higher living standards which it as surely demonstrates.

The needs of the productive forces plus the rebelliousness of the peasantry would not by themselves have been sufficient to break the yoke of landlordism and imperialism. Three other factors helped:

(1) The weakening of world imperialism as a result of increasing contradictions between the powers, and the paralysis affecting their mutual intervention brought about by the existence of the H-bomb.

(2) The growing importance of the state in backward countries. It is one of the tricks of history that when a historical task faces society, and the class that traditionally carries it out is absent, some other group of people, quite often a state power, implements it. State power, under such conditions, plays a very important role. It reflects not only, or even mainly, the national economic base on which it rises,

but the supra-national character of the world economy today.

(3) The growing importance of the intelligentsia as the leader and unifier of the nation, and above all as manipulator of the masses. This last point will need special elaboration.

The intelligentsia

The revolutionary intelligentsia has proved itself a much more cohesive factor in the emergent nations of today than in Tsarist Russia. Quite understandably bourgeois private property is bankrupt; imperialism is intolerable; state capitalism—through the weakening of imperialism, the growing importance of state planning, plus the example of Russia, and the organised disciplined work of the Communist parties—gives them a new sense of cohesion. As the only non-specialised section of society, the intelligentsia is the obvious source of a 'professional revolutionary elite' which appears to represent the interests of the 'nation' as against conflicting sectional and class interests. In addition, it is the section of society most imbued with the national culture, the peasants and workers having neither the leisure nor education for it.

The intelligentsia is also sensitive to their countries' technical lag. Participating as they do in the scientific and technical world of the 20th century, they are stifled by the backwardness of their own nation. This feeling is accentuated by the 'intellectual unemployment' endemic in these countries. Given the general economic backwardness, the only hope for most students is a government job, but there are not nearly enough of these to go round.

They are great believers in efficiency, including efficiency in social engineering. They hope for reform from above and would dearly love to hand the new world over to a grateful people, rather than see the liberating struggle of a self-conscious and freely associated people result in a new world for themselves. They care a lot for measures to drag their nation out of stagnation, but very little for democracy. They embody the drive for industrialisation, for capital accumulation, for national resurgence. Their power is in direct relation to the feebleness of other classes, and their political nullity.

All this makes totalitarian state capitalism a very attractive goal for intellectuals. And indeed they are the main banner-bearers of Communism in the emergent nations. 'Communism has found greatest acceptance in Latin America among students and the middle class,' writes a Latin American specialist. In India, at the Congress of the Communist Party in Amritsar (March/April 1958), 'approximately 67 percent of the delegates were from classes other than the proletariat and peasantry (middle class, land-owning class, and 'small traders'); 72 percent had some college education.'

Deflected permanent revolution

Those forces which should lead to a socialist workers' revolution according to Trotsky's theory can lead, in the absence of the revolutionary subject, the proletariat, to its opposite, state capitalism. Using what is of universal validity in the theory and what is contingent (upon the subjective activity of the proletariat), one can come to a variant that, for lack of a better name, might be called the 'deflected, state capitalist, permanent revolution.'

The collapse of the Stalinist regimes in Russia and Eastern Europe, the move of Mao's China onto the rails of market capitalism, the disintegration of the Stalinist and Maoist movements internationally, are opening the path for the development of authentic permanent revolution as described by Trotsky.

We are in the midst of a long, slow awakening of the working class movement in the Third World.

We have seen the working class of Iran involved in a general strike and organised in the *shoras* (workers' councils) leading to the overthrow of the Shah. We have seen the working class of South Africa smashing the apartheid regime. We have witnessed the emergence of a militant working class movement in South Korea. We have also witnessed the largest mass general strike ever in Brazil.

It will take time to overcome the depression left by decades of reaction, of Stalinism and fascism. But the path is open for the authentic permanent revolution to come into its own.

Chapter 7

Marxism on oppression

The heart of Marxism is that the emancipation of the working class is the act of the working class itself. At the same time Marx argues that the prevailing ideas in society are the ideas of the ruling class. One important form these ideas take is the break-up of the unity of workers into different races, nationalities and gender.

Oppression of blacks by whites, of women by men, etc, divides the working class, and the policy of divide and rule strengthens the power of the capitalists.

How does the oppression affect the condition of workers who belong to the oppressed section? Black workers in Britain are exploited as workers. Being discriminated against as blacks sharpens the exploitation. They get lower wages, their conditions at work are worse, they suffer from bad housing and other social deprivations. The same applies to women workers, who are forced to suffer a double burden of earning wages plus looking after the children and the house. Their jobs are very much more marginal; they have less opportunity for attaining skills; they are forced to give up work to look after the young children; their oppression sharpens their exploitation.

How does the oppression affect workers who belong to the oppressing section? Of course they believe they are superior to the 'inferior' workers. But do they really benefit from this? White workers in the Southern states of the US think they benefit because they earn more than the blacks, have better housing, and so on. But white workers earn far more in the North; in fact blacks in the North earn more than Southern whites.

Protestant workers in Northern Ireland may think that beating the Catholics is good for them, otherwise they would not do it. So the Protestant worker is more likely to have a job and be better off than the Catholic worker, but the same worker earns less than a worker in Birmingham or Glasgow.

The same applies to the relations between a male and female worker. He earns more than her, therefore on the face of it he benefits from her oppression. But this is a very shallow view of the situation. Think about it. A male worker writes to his friend, 'Have you heard the marvellous news? My wife gets peanuts in wages, the nursery costs the earth, her job is under threat all the time, and to put the cap on it, she is pregnant again and there are no means to get an abortion. Marvellous news!'

If I'm travelling on a filthy dirty train, as a white man under capitalism I will have a seat next to the window. The woman or the black will have a seat away from the window in even worse conditions than me. But the real problem is the train. We all have to endure the same train. We have no control over a driver who is taking us all into the abyss.

The most oppressed section of the working class always reflects the extreme horrors of capitalism. Trotsky once wrote that if one wants to grasp the need for change to a new society, one needs to look through the eyes of women. If one wants to grasp the nature of decaying, senile capitalism, one needs to look since the last world war, through the eyes of Jews. If one wants to grasp the nature of British society today, one needs to look through the eyes of Neville and Doreen Lawrence, the parents of Stephen Lawrence, the black youth murdered by five Nazis, the latter protected by the British police.

To achieve unity between white and black workers the white workers must move toward the black workers and go a mile further. To achieve unity between male and female workers, the male worker must go out of his way to prove that he is not part of the oppressors. Lenin put it very simply in 1902. He wrote that when workers go on strike for higher wages they are simply trade unionists. Only when they go on strike against the beating of Jews or of students are they really socialists.

A strike involving black and white workers helps to undermine racism. A strike strengthens solidarity, and therefore has an impact beyond the immediate issue. The spiritual changes in workers is the most precious result of the strike.

But solidarity can start from an anti-racist demonstration that leads to a feeling of unity with black workers that has an impact on future industrial disputes. The meetings in London in solidarity with the Lawrences are very large, composed of black and white people, and no doubt will have a big impact not only on the attitude of millions to the police but also will inspire increasing solidarity among workers on a whole number of other issues.

A strike in which men and women stand shoulder to shoulder helps to overcome sexism. One should remember the Paris Commune where the women fought brilliantly, causing one British reporter to say that if all the Communards were women they would have won.

In a meeting in London a short while ago I said, 'Come the revolution, and the chairperson of the workers' council in London will be a young black woman aged 26, and a lesbian.' I chose these characteristics because all of them break the taboos of capitalism. Young is bad. Black is bad. Woman is bad. Lesbian is bad. After the meeting a young black woman approached me and said, 'That's me. I am black, I'm a woman, as you can see, I am aged 26 and I'm a lesbian.' I said to her, 'I'm sorry, sister, you have missed the boat. The revolution will be in ten years time. You'll be too old.' Of course my words should not be taken literally. The chairperson of the London workers' council can be an Irishman aged 70, a grandfather of 15 kids.

A revolutionary has to be extreme in opposition to all forms of oppression. A white revolutionary must be more extreme in opposing racism than a black revolutionary. A gentile revolutionary must oppose anti-Semitism more strongly than any Jew. A male revolutionary must be completely intolerant of any harassment or belittling of women. We must be the tribune of the oppressed.

Chapter 8

The struggle against fascism

Lessons of Nazi victory in 1933

On 30 January 1933 Hitler became the prime minister of Germany. This was not inevitable at all. Two months earlier, in November 1932, the Social Democratic Party (SPD) won 7.2 million votes and the Communist Party (KPD) 6 million. So the two organisations between them got 13.2 million votes, while the Nazi vote was 11.7 million, ie 1.5 million votes less. Even more significant was the quality of the supporters of the workers' organisations as against those of the Nazis. As Trotsky put it:

> On the scales of election statistics, 1,000 fascist votes weigh as much as 1,000 Communist votes. But on the scales of the revolutionary struggle, 1,000 workers in one big factory represent a force 100 times greater than 1,000 petty officials, clerks, their wives and their mothers-in-law. The great bulk of the fascists consists of human dust.

Alas, the leadership of the two mass organisations was completely bankrupt.

In the face of the menace of Nazism the SPD relied on the German state and its police to defend democracy. Even after Hitler had become prime minister, Otto Wels, leader of the SPD, could state that people should not be worried: the new cabinet was not purely National Socialist but only a coalition of German Nationalists with National Socialists; only three of the 12 government members were Nazis, the other nine being Conservative. Moreover, Hitler had promised the president on oath to uphold the Weimar Constitution. And Wilhelm Frick, the Nazi minister of the interior, had announced that the cabinet had refused to ban the Communist Party and would not interfere with the freedom of the press! A couple of months later, of course, the Communist Party was banned, and Socialist candidates to the elections were arrested.

When on 23 March 1933 an enabling law giving Hitler unlimited power was moved at the Reichstag, Otto Wels spoke against it, but he made it clear that the party, acting as a lawful opposition, would only offer non-violent, lawful opposition to the regime. Wels said:

> The election of 5 March has given a majority to the government parties and thereby given them a chance to govern according to the text and spirit of the constitution... We accept their present rule as a fact. However, the people's sense of justice is also a political force, and we shall not cease to appeal to this sense of justice.

The KPD leadership was not less bankrupt. In Stalin's footsteps they declared that the Social Democrats were social fascists, ie there was no qualitative difference between the Nazis and Social Democracy. Hence Remmele, leader of the KPD Reichstag faction, could declare on 14 October 1931 that after Hitler it would be Remmele's turn. 'We are not afraid of the fascist gentlemen. They will shoot their bolt quicker than any other government. (Right you are! From the Communists.)'

Trotsky, with all his passion and brilliance, called on German workers to face the threatening catastrophe represented by Hitler. On 23 November he wrote a pamphlet entitled 'Germany, the Key to the International Situation'. He said:

> On the direction in which the solution of the German crisis develops will depend not only the fate of Germany herself (and that is already a great deal), but also the fate of Europe, the destiny of the entire world, for many years to come... The coming to power of the National Socialists would mean first of all the extermination of the flower of the German proletariat, the destruction of its organisations, the eradication of its belief in itself and in its future. Considering the far greater maturity and acuteness of the social contradictions in Germany, the hellish work of Italian Fascism would probably appear as a pale and almost humane experiment in comparison with the work of the German National Socialists... Ten proletarian insurrections, ten defeats, one on top of the other, could not debilitate and enfeeble the German working class as much as a retreat before fascism would weaken it at the very moment when the decision is still impending on the question of who is to become master in the German household... the key to the world situation lies in Germany.

Three days after Trotsky wrote 'Germany, the Key to the International Situation', he wrote another strong appeal and warning to

German workers entitled 'For a Workers' United Front Against Fascism'. He wrote the following urgent words:

> Communist workers, you are hundreds of thousands, millions; you cannot leave for any place; there are not enough passports for you. Should fascism come to power, it will ride over your skulls and spines like a terrific tank. Your salvation lies in merciless struggle. And only a fighting unity with the Social Democratic workers can bring victory. Make haste, Communist workers, you have very little time left!

On 28 May 1933, in an article entitled 'The German Catastrophe: the Responsibilities of the Leadership', he wrote again, 'The unparalleled defeat of the German proletariat is the most important event since the conquest of power by the Russian proletariat.' And on 22 June 1933 he concluded, 'The present catastrophe in Germany is undoubtedly the greatest defeat of the working class in history.'

We in the SWP have learnt the lessons of Germany

With the coming to office of Labour in 1974 unemployment rose from 600,000 to 1.6 million three years later. Wages fell, and for the first time since the war there was a decline in the real standard of living. With poverty and deprivation the conditions existed for the growth of the Nazi National Front (NF). In 1976 the NF got 44,000 votes in the local elections. The National Party, the other Nazi Party, gained two council seats in Blackburn. In 1977, in the elections to the Greater London Council, the NF got 119,063 votes (5 percent, compared with 0.5 percent in 1973), beating the Liberals into third place in 33 constituencies. An Essex University survey suggested the NF support during this period would give it 25 MPs under proportional representation.

In August 1977 the NF organised a march through Lewisham, a borough in south east London with a big black population. The SWP brought 2,000 of their members and mobilised locally another 8,000 or so workers and youth, mainly black, together with whom they broke through the police cordon and physically stopped the fascist march.

The SWP activity in Lewisham was denounced by practically all the spokesmen of the Labour Party. Michael Foot, then deputy prime minister, said, 'You don't stop the Nazis by throwing bottles or bashing the police. The most ineffective way of fighting the fascists is to behave like them.' Ron Hayward, general secretary of the Labour Party, appealed to all its members to keep away from extreme left and extreme right organisations. He saw little difference between the violent demonstrators (ie SWP) and 'NF fascists'.

The events in Lewisham in August 1977 acted as a springboard for the founding of the Anti Nazi League in November 1977.

The ANL was a united front set up by the Socialist Workers' Party, Peter Hain and Labour MP Ernie Roberts and, among other MPs, Neil Kinnock, Audrey Wise and Martin Flannery, who were on the left of the party.

The ANL became an immensely popular movement. To give a focus for youth against the NF—the age group they drew most of their support from—the ANL organised its first Carnival in London at the end of April 1979, before the local elections. Its success was beyond everyone's expectations, bringing 80,000 on a march from Trafalgar Square to a music festival in Victoria Park six miles away. Together with Rock Against Racism huge carnivals were organised in Manchester (35,000), Cardiff (5,000), Edinburgh (8,000), Harwich (2,000), Southampton (5,000), Bradford (2,000) and London again (100,000) The NF vote in the subsequent local elections collapsed. In Leeds it declined by 54 percent, in Bradford by 77 percent; even in its heartland of the East End of London it dropped by 40 percent.

The ANL was widely sponsored by unions. As early as mid-April 1978, before the Carnival, there were 30 AUEW branches and districts sponsoring it, 25 trades councils, 11 NUM areas and lodges, six to ten branches from the TGWU, CPSA, TASS, NUJ, NUT and NUPE, 13 shop stewards' committees in major factories, and 50 local Labour Parties. Numbers grew after the Carnivals.

Under the hammer of the ANL the fascists never managed to have a resurgence of support to get nearer to what it was in 1976-77. To repeat, in 1976 the NF got 44,000 votes in Leicester and a year later 119,000 votes in London. In the last local elections in England, on 17 May 1998, the total vote of the British National Party and National Front was only 3,000.

Our policy of fighting fascism was two-track: attacking the rats and attacking the sewers in which the rats multiply. Fighting the fascists is not enough. One has also to fight the unemployment, low wages and social deprivation that create conditions for the growth of fascism. One demonstration of the unity of the two tracks was organising nurses in uniform to canvass against the Nazis and in defence of the National Health Service.

Comparison with SOS Racisme in France

In the elections in 1974 the Front National (FN) got a mere 0.74 percent of the vote; in 1981 it was even lower, 0.5 percent. But with the election of the Socialist François Mitterrand to the presidency in 1981 things changed radically. The disappointment was massive. Unemployment more than doubled. The FN mushroomed. In 1984 it polled 11 percent of the votes or about 2 million. In the March 1986 parliamentary elections it won 35 MPs, as many as the Communist Party. Since then the electoral system changed and the FN has no MPs but it has over 1,000 councillors, and controls four smallish towns in southern France. In the last general election of June 1997 the FN won 5 million votes, or 15 percent of the total vote.

Why is the curve of the NF in Britain radically downwards, while that in France moves sharply upwards? One cannot explain it by referring to differences in the objective situations of France and Britain.

The proportion of blacks in Britain is similar to that in France, 5 to 6 percent. Unemployment levels are not different. The level of industrial struggle has been much higher in France, in fact, than Britain. Britain had suffered the longest and deepest downturn in industrial struggle.

So how to explain the difference between the fates of the FN and NF? One has to look to the subjective element. In Britain we have the ANL. In France the main organisation against the Nazis has been SOS Racisme. This organisation is the coat-tail of the Socialist Party. Its leader, Harlem Desir, argues against 'confrontation' with the FN, claiming this will 'play into Le Pen's hands'. He looks to public opinion to uproot racism and expects equal contributions from left and right wing organisations. Though SOS Racisme calls demonstrations, these are not designed to physically confront the FN.

The role of Mitterrand in castrating SOS Racisme was central. One must remember that Mitterrand was a high official in Marshal Pétain's government during the war, a government that collaborated with the Nazis, delivering 70,000 Jews to the gas chambers. After Mitterrand became president, every year, on the anniversary of Marshal

Pétain's death, he put a wreath on the grave of this 'great French patriot'. Another wreath was laid on the same grave by Le Pen.

Chapter 9

Important lessons from the May 1968 events

Inspiration and warning

Socialists throughout the world were inspired by the events in France in May 1968. Student demonstrations and occupations of the universities culminated on 10-11 May—the Night of the Barricades— with a massive confrontation between thousands of students, aided by numerous young workers and inhabitants of the Latin Quarter, and the CRS, the riot police, whom they successfully repulsed.

The French Communist Party, which had extremely strong support, opposed the student activities until the Night of the Barricades. Now they decided that the best way to face the rising wave was to put themselves at the head of the movement. The leaders of the Communist Party and CGT union federation hoped that a one-day strike and demonstration would serve as a safety valve. So they called a one-day strike for the 13 May. They expected it to be a token strike like the many token strikes they had called before. But they were wrong. Rank and file workers took the initiative to prolong the strike. On 14 May the workers of Sud Aviation in Nantes declared an unlimited strike and occupied the factory. The next day, the 15th, Renault-Cleon was occupied. On 16 May the strike and occupation movement spread to all the Renault factories. This was followed by a strike and occupation throughout all the engineering factories, the car and aeroplane plants. On 19 May the trams stopped, along with mail and telegraph services. The Metro and bus services in Paris followed suit. The strike hit the mines, shipping, Air France, etc. On 20 May the strike became general, involving ten million workers. People who had never struck before were involved: Folies Bergère dancers, soccer players, journalists, saleswomen, technicians. Red flags decorated all workplaces.

In the demonstration of the 13th a million people participated, workers and students.

President de Gaulle was completely helpless. When on 24 May he called for a referendum, he could not find one printshop in France ready to print his ballot papers, and when, in desperation, he tried to have the ballot papers printed in Belgium, the Belgian workers refused, in solidarity with their French brethren. On 29 May de Gaulle fled France to find refuge with the French troops in Germany.

Alas, the high tide of workers' struggle ended.

On 27 May the union leaders signed the Grenelle Agreement offering big economic concessions to workers, eg a rise of 35 percent for lower paid workers.

The strike was called off, the right gained the initiative and began to mobilise, a massive demonstration of the right took place on 30 May. The police seized the TV and radio stations, threw out the occupying workers, attacked any continuing demonstrations and even killed two workers and a school student.

'The tradition of the dead generations hangs like a nightmare on the mind of the living' (Marx)

Throughout the massive forward movement of the workers, the dead weight of Stalinism made its impact felt. French workers had great loyalty to the Communist Party. After all, a generation of workers was educated and trained by the party. One event in the past shows the power of the CP over the workers. When the US and British armies defeated the German army, Paris was liberated by the Maqui, the resistance movement led by the Communist Party. Armed workers controlled Paris. Then Maurice Thorez, general secretary of the French Communist Party, flew from Moscow to Paris and announced, ' One police, one army, one state.' The police Thorez referred to were the police who had collaborated with the Nazis throughout the war. Still, the workers of Paris accepted Thorez's instruction, and they were disarmed.

Now, in May 1968, the impact of the Communist Party was absolutely massive.

We mentioned the 1 million workers and students who demonstrated in Paris. The CP leaders did not want the workers and students to mix, as the students were far freer from the influence of the Communist Party; their political ideas were far to the left of the party. So the CP leaders organised a chain of 20,000 stewards to separate the workers' bloc from the students' bloc.

We mentioned the factory occupations. Here again the role of the CP and CGT bureaucracy was decisive: 80-90 percent of the workers were sent home, so that only a minority were active in the occupation. The isolated workers at home of course lost the opportunity to discuss tactics and strategy, the spirit of the movement.

The strikes had strike committees, but these were not elected by the workers but appointed by the union officials.

To facilitate the ending of the general strike, workers in one factory were told that workers in another factory had already gone back to work, and this tactic was repeated over and over again. As there was no line of communication between factories independent of the union machine, this tactic worked.

The February 1917 revolution in Russia

To understand the contradictions in workers' consciousness in May 1968 in France one can do no better than look at the experience of the February Revolution in Russia in 1917. This revolution put an end to Tsarism. The police completely dissolved. Workers were organised in soviets everywhere. In the army soldiers' committees mushroomed

Lenin at the time coined the words 'dual power' as dominating the situation in Russia. It is true that the soviets were powerful, but parallel to the soviets was the bourgeois Provisional Government. It is true there were soldiers' committees, but still the generals commanded the army. It is true that the soviets expressed the wish of the millions for peace, but the imperialist war continued. It is true that powerful workers' committees existed in every factory, but still every factory was owned by the capitalists. It is true that millions of peasants were organised in soviets, but still the landlord did not lose one square yard of their land. The leadership of the soviets, the Mensheviks and Social Revolutionaries, supported the bourgeois government and its policies.

The February Revolution was a break with the past, but not a complete break. Contradictions existed in the institutions of the time, and in the consciousness of the millions.

The Petrograd Soviet was a fantastic new institution, but it was not led by the Bolsheviks. The right wing dominated it. For millions of people who yesterday had supported Tsarism, a break from Tsarism, a move to the left, did not bring them straight away to Bolshevism, but the right of them, to the Mensheviks and Social Revolutionaries. It took weeks and months of struggle for the Bolsheviks to win the soviets of Petrograd and Moscow, in September 1917. We have no space to describe the different events between February and October. It was not a straightforward march of Bolshevism. The Bolshevik influence increased in Petrograd until the end of June. At the beginning of July they were pushed right back, the party was made practically illegal, its press was smashed, Lenin was forced to go into hiding and Trotsky was imprisoned. July was, as Trotsky wrote, the month of slander, the press coming out hysterically in its denunciation of Lenin as a German agent. The swing to the right gave confidence to the extreme rightists, and on 27-30 August General Kornilov, commander-in-chief of the Russian army, launched a coup. Had he won, the word for fascism would not have been an Italian but a Russian word. From inside prison Trotsky organised the defence of Petrograd against Kornilov. The defeat of Kornilov massively speeded up the forward march of Bolshevism. Days afterwards the Bolsheviks got their majority in the soviets of Petrograd and Moscow, and a few weeks later the October Revolution took place.

The revolution is not a one-day event. It is a process. Workers have to break with the bourgeois ideas that dominated before, but this break is not completed in one day. For a time a contradictory consciousness exists among workers. Of course the slogan of the Bolsheviks from April, 'Land, bread and peace. All power to the soviets', was a consistent slogan to solve the problems facing the millions of peasants who wanted land, the hungry millions who needed bread, the millions tormented by the war. But for a time many workers said, 'Yes, of course we want the land, but we should wait until the war is over and parliament passes a law giving us the land.' Of course we want peace, but let us be victorious in the war first and then get peace.

The Bolshevik Party in March 1917 had 23,000 members, and having the support of 2.5 percent of the soviets they had a strong enough springboard to move forward to victory.

The left alternative to the French Communist Party was minuscule.

The total number of Trotskyists in France in May 1968 was 400. The number of organised Maoists was of a similar size. This was far too few to challenge the Stalinists. Had the Trotskyists had a few tens of thousand of members they could have argued effectively in the 13 May demonstration of 1 million for workers and students to join hands, breaking the cordon formed by the 20,000 stewards. In the occupied factories they could have argued with the workers to stay in the factories and not go home, which would have given them the ability to take initiatives. They could have argued for the election of strike committees instead of accepting the nominated committees. They would have been able to create communication between the factories so that the bureaucracy could not use the policy of divide and rule to call the strike off.

The coming May 1968 events

A mass explosion is inevitable in the future. Of course one never knows in advance when exactly it will happen. After all, Lenin, three weeks before the February Revolution, speaking to a group of Young Socialists in Switzerland, finished his description and analysis of the 1905 revolution saying that they, the youth, would see the Russian Revolution, but not his older generation. A few days before the revolution (7 February) Lenin wrote to his friend Inessa Armand, 'Yesterday there was a meeting (meetings tire me; nerves no good at all; headaches; left before the end).' Had he known that a few days later the revolution was to start he would not have complained in this manner.

The great turning points can never be foreseen, for obvious reasons. For a long time history moves very slowly. Over ten or 20 years there are only molecular changes, and then, suddenly, in a day or a week, changes greater than over generations take place.

The contradictions in capitalism today are much sharper than they were in 1968. The year 1968 was towards the end of the longest boom in the history of capitalism. Since 1973 one recession has followed another. The instability of capitalism is greater than ever, workers' exploitation and insecurity grows by the day. Great explosions are absolutely inevitable. But for these explosions to end in a proletarian victory, the need for a revolutionary party is greater than ever. The mass of the workers' spontaneous action is like steam. The revolutionary party is like a piston. A piston by itself is useless, steam by itself disperses futily. For a proletarian victory the question of leadership is crucial. May 1968 should be both an inspiration for us and a warning.

Chapter 10

The Russian Revolution

On 23 February 1917 celebrations of International Women's Day began. This was the start of the revolution. Next day 200,000 workers went on strike in Petrograd. The day after, on the 25th, a general strike gripped the city and a number of strikers were killed by the army. Two days later there was a mutiny of the Guards regiments, soldiers refused to shoot at demonstrators, and in some cases, the officer ordering the shootings was killed by one of the soldiers. The Tsar abdicated. What is interesting is that just a day before the abdication of the Tsar a Soviet of Workers' Deputies was formed. The memory of the 1905 Soviet accelerated the event. All workplaces sent delegates to the Soviet.

The revolution was completely spontaneous and unplanned. As Trotsky correctly stated:

> No one, positively no one—we can assert this categorically upon the basis of all the data—then thought that 23 February was to mark the beginning of a decisive drive against absolutism.

Sukhanov, a brilliant witness of the revolution, observes, 'Not one party was preparing for the great upheaval.' Similarly a former director of the *okhrana*, the Tsarist secret police, stated that the revolution was 'a purely spontaneous phenomenon, and not at all the fruit of party agitation.' As millions of people came into political life for the first time, the Bolshevik Party appeared as very marginal, having, after the revolution, some 23,000 members. It was not until 25 February that the Bolsheviks came out with their first leaflet calling for a general strike—after 200,000 workers had already downed tools! In the elections to the soviet the Bolsheviks made up a tiny minority. Out of 1,500 to 1,600 delegates only 40, or 2.5 percent were Bolsheviks.

Dual power

Side by side with the Provisional Government, led by Prince L'vov, was the government of the soviets. There was, therefore, dual power.

Such a situation could not continue for any length of time. One of the two governments would have to give way.

To start with, the Soviet supported the L'vov government. At the session of the Soviet of 2 March, a resolution was put forward to transfer power to the Provisional Government, ie to the bourgeoisie. Only 15 deputies voted against it. This means that not even the 40 Bolsheviks opposed this. The mass pressure from some 1,600 deputies bent the Bolsheviks over. The parties dominating the Soviet, the Mensheviks and Social Revolutionaries, took a muddled position. They supported the soviets but also supported the bourgeois Provisional Government. They wanted peace but supported the war. They were sympathetic to the peasants' demand for land but supported the government which was the spokesman of the landowners.

But a revolution does not allow a middle way compromise. Life posed every question in very extreme form.

The Bolshevik leadership in Russia were themselves extremely muddled. On 3 March the Petrograd Committee of the Bolshevik Party passed a resolution that it would 'not oppose the power of the Provisional Government in so far as its activities correspond to the interests of the proletariat and of the broad democratic masses of the people.' The formula 'in so far as' (*postolka, posilku*) appeared in the resolution of the Executive Committee of the Petrograd Soviet on relations with the Provisional Government, and became a way of referring to this particular policy of supporting the government.

Lenin in Switzerland was livid when he got a copy of *Pravda* that declared that the Bolsheviks would decisively support the Provisional Government 'insofar as it struggles against reaction or counter-revolution'—forgetting that the only important agent of counter-revolution at the time was this same Provisional Government.

Lenin rearms the party

On 3 April 1917 Lenin arrived in Petrograd. When Lenin arrived at the Finland station the Bolshevik Party supported the victorious February Revolution. Lenin was contemptuous and raised the slogans, 'Bread, peace and land', and, 'All power to the soviets.'

The revolutionaries of course tried to influence the masses, but it is not a one-way street. The views of the massive majority affect the revolutionaries. A few days later Lenin met the Petrograd committee of the Bolshevik Party. He argued the case for his April Theses. Out of 16 members present, two voted to support Lenin, 13 voted against, and one abstained.

In spite of this inauspicious beginning, Lenin was able to win a large proportion of the party to his stand in an astonishingly short time. This was the result both of Lenin's consistency and the daily experience of millions. The war went on, thousands continued to die, the landlords still harshly exploited the peasants, the capitalists lived a life of luxury while the workers suffered from penury. It took something like a month for Lenin to win the party over.

To win the soviets to his viewpoint took a little longer. At the beginning of September the Bolsheviks won a majority in the soviet of Petrograd and Trotsky became its president. At the same time the Bolsheviks won the soviet in Moscow, and the Bolshevik Kamenev became its president.

From this it was a short haul to the victory of the October Revolution.

While the February Revolution was spontaneous, the October Revolution was planned.

On 10 October the Central Committee of the Bolshevik Party declared for an armed insurrection. Three days later the soldiers' section of the Petrograd Soviet voted to transfer all military authority from headquarters to a Military Revolutionary Committee headed by Trotsky. On 16 October an enlarged plenum of the Central Committee, the Executive Commission of the Petrograd Committee, the Military Organisation, members of the Petrograd Soviet, trade unions, factory committees, the Petrograd Area Committee and the railwaymen reaffirmed the decision on the insurrection. On 20 October the Military Revolutionary Committee began actual preparations for the insurrection. On 25 October the insurrection took place. Trotsky organised this action brilliantly, as he did later when he led the Red Army to victory in the civil war.

Because the October Revolution was so well planned and executed hardly any blood was spilt. Far more people lost their lives in the February Revolution.

Following the revolution, during the civil war, many hundreds of thousands were killed. But this was not because of the action of the Soviet government, but because of the invasion of some 16 foreign armies. To blame the Bolsheviks for this would be like blaming any person defending himself from a murderer for using violence.

Victorious revolution

Throughout the 20th century there were a number of proletarian revolutions. Alas, only one of them—the 1917 Russian Revolution—ended in victory. Again and again we witness half-carried revolutions, which confirm the prophetic words of St Just at the time of the French Revolution: 'Those who make half a revolution dig their own grave.'

The Russian Revolution of 1917 was an exception to the series of half-made revolutions. The Bolshevik Party played a crucial role in the completion of the Russian Revolution.

The difference between success and failure, between Russia in October 1917 and the other workers' revolutions, was that in the former case there was a mass revolutionary party providing effective leadership. While socialists cannot determine the moment when the revolutionary crisis breaks, they do determine the eventual outcome by the degree to which they build a strong revolutionary party.

The working class, not the party, makes the revolution, but the party guides the working class,' Trotsky aptly wrote. 'Without a guiding organisation the energy of the masses would dissipate like steam not enclosed in a piston box. But nevertheless what moves things is not the piston or the box, but the steam.'

The land of the landowners was distributed to the peasants, the factories were taken into state ownership and were run under workers' control, the oppressed nationalities got the right of self determination, and Russia that was a prison of nations became a federation of free and equal peoples.

For centuries anti-Semitism was rampant in Tsarist Russia. In 1881 500 pogroms were carried out against Jews. Jews were not allowed to live in the two capitals, Moscow and St Petrograd, unless they got special permission. Now the president of the soviet of Petrograd was a Jew, Trotsky, the president of the soviet of Moscow was a Jew, Kamenev, and the president of the Soviet Republic was a Jew, Sverdlov. When Trotsky moved to be the head of the Red Army he was replaced as president of the Petrograd Soviet by another Jew, Zinoviev.

The revolution was a festival of the oppressed. During 1917, during the month of the revolution Anatoly Lunacharsky, a brilliant speaker, held meetings of 30,000 to 40,000 people, and he would speak for two to three hours on subjects like William Shakespeare, Greek drama, etc. The population of London is four times greater than Petrograd at that time, and British workers are more literate than the Russians were. But in no way could one see a similar meeting held in London.

The Soviet government enacted the most progressive legislation in the world aiming at the emancipation of women: the right of divorce at the instigation of only one partner; free abortion on demand (the first in the world); communal feeding to free women from the kitchen; the communal upbringing of children. Also all laws against gays were got rid of.

Didn't the Russian Revolution lead to Stalin and the gulag?

This argument is heard so many times by opponents of the revolution. And it sounds like common sense. Alas, it is the same common sense that could say: the atomic bomb on Hiroshima was the product of Newton's law of gravity. There is an element of truth: if not for the law of gravity the bomb would not fall down from the plane.

The key to understanding the rise of Stalin is in the international nature of the Russian Revolution.

The Russian Revolution was part of world revolution, and cannot be explained other than in terms of international factors. The Russian industrial working class was tiny: the number of workers in the factories, railways and mines was only three million out of a population of 160 million. The industrial output of Russia in 1917 was not greater than that of tiny Belgium. But the working class was much more concentrated in big units. Thus, for instance, there were 40,000 workers in the Putilov engineering factory; it was the largest factory in the world at the time. This was not the product of the gradual organic development of the Russian economy: it was overwhelmingly the result of foreign capital invested in Russia.

The aspirations of Russian workers were also shaped by international conditions. In Britain it took more than two centuries from the beginning of factory production to workers being imbued with the demand for the eight hour day. In Russia it became the central demand of the 1905 revolution.

Marxism was also not a native product of Russia. There was no

Russian Adam Smith followed by a Russian David Ricardo followed by a Russian Karl Marx. Marxism came fully fledged into the intellectual-political life of Russia. Volume I of *Capital* was published first in 1867. It appeared in the Russian edition six years later. It was the first language into which *Capital* was translated. Finally, the last impetus for the Russian Revolution also came from abroad—the hammering by the German troops of the Russian army.

Lenin and Trotsky again and again warned that the Soviet regime would be doomed if the Revolution did not spread, above all if the German Revolution did not come to its aid. And so it came to be.

Stalin was not the heir of the Russian Revolution, but its gravedigger. The fact that he murdered every member of the Bolshevik Central Committee who survived the revolution and the civil war demonstrates this. The father of Stalinism was not Lenin but Noske, the right wing Social Democratic leader who was directly involved in the murder of Rosa Luxemburg and Karl Liebknecht, and in the murder of the German Revolution.

Tragically, the German Revolution was far less well organised or developed than the Russian. I remember meeting Heinrich Brändler, leader of the German Communist Party after the death of Rosa Luxemburg. I asked him what the state of Rosa Luxemburg's organisation was in 1918. He said it had some 4,000 members, the majority of them not Marxists but pacifists (his words). Compare this to the Bolsheviks, who existed as a party since 1903, with a membership in 1917 of 23,600—and this in a country where the working class was much smaller than in Germany.

In a stream water remains clean. In stagnating water, scum comes to the top. The isolation of the Russian Revolution led to the bureaucratic scum coming to the top. And when Stalin entered into competition with Western imperialism, he of necessity imitated it. If Nazi Germany had a massive industrial-military machine, Stalin wanted the same. To achieve this quickly, the only way was by harshly exploiting the Russian workers and peasants—hence the gulag. Stalinist Russia became more and more symmetrical to Nazi Germany. Its regime became state capitalist.

Chapter 11

Capitalism and militarism

Turkey spends half of its state budget on arms. It has become a major military power in the region. Nowadays the government is pushing wage restraint and privatisation policies, while on the other hand spending huge amounts of money on tanks and helicopters.

During the last two weeks arms spending has become an important item of discussion even in the bosses' papers. One columnist has written that 'for every Turkish citizen there is only half an aspirin tablet (a cheap medicine for headaches) but three hand bombs. For every 10,000 people there is only one health centre but two tanks.' The Turkish army is the largest unit of NATO with the exception of the United States, although Turkey's national income is much smaller than those of Germany, France, Britain or Italy.

The changing role of the arms economy

In different periods of capitalism the war industry played different roles. When capitalism was young and progressive the army played a subordinate role. But things changed when capitalism entered into its decline. In Germany in 1933 unemployment reached eight million. A couple of years later Nazi rearmament got rid of unemployment. This was followed by the same thing happening in the United States, Britain and other capitalist countries.

After the end of the war, the Cold War kept the standing army at a much higher level than in the 1920s and early 1930s, but of course much lower than in the war years. This was what we called at the time the permanent arms economy. It kept employment high, but it was full of contradictions. In 1956, in an article entitled 'The Permanent War Economy', I explained those contradictions. Spending on arms encourages full employment, but leads to a situation in which a country that spends a lot on arms would find itself unable to spend as much on retooling industry as countries that spend far less on defence. This became obvious in the 1960s and early 1970s. The Cold War and spending on arms kept employment high. But countries like

Japan and West Germany which were spending very little on defence, showed their ability to retool industry much better than the United States or Britain. West Germany and Japan won the competition in the car industry, electronics and other fields of the economy. The collapse of the dollar with the accompanying massive rise in the price of oil in 1973 forced the United States and Britain to cut their military budget drastically.

No simple relation between capitalism and militarism

It is true that militarism serves capitalism, but this does not mean to say that the generals have no interests of their own that they try to impose on society. If a capitalist, in defence of his interests, employs a gangster, this does not mean that the gangster has no interests of his own that he will try to impose on his master. The economy is the base, and the military and politics are in the superstructure. But the superstructure has an influence on the base. The Turkish generals are fighting to keep a massive army, far beyond what many of the Turkish capitalists would like. When the earthquake in north west Turkey took place, the army rushed quickly to the scene, not with spades or bulldozers to remove the rubble in order to save the number of people buried alive, but they rushed to impose law and order using machine guns and tanks. The generals have their own agenda as regards the Turkish working class and the oppressed nationalities. They will try to impose their will on society.

Chapter 12

Democratic revolution or socialist revolution?

In all countries that have no political democracy—ie countries which are dominated by an absolute monarchy, or the army, or fascism, or a foreign imperialist power—the need for democracy is obvious. And we, revolutionary socialists, fight hard to achieve this: free elections of national and local governments, freedom of the press, of assembly and organisation, the right of national self determination. But this is not enough for us.

First of all, inequality, exploitation and oppression still remain intact so long as the wealth is in the hands of a tiny minority of capitalists. Without the common ownership of the means of production, not only does inequality between rich and poor remain, but also, because of the competition between workers for jobs, housing, educational opportunities, the inequality inside the working class remains. This is a breeding ground for racism and sexism.

With the continued control of the wealth of society by the capitalists, political democracy is also unsafe, and the old political order threatens to return. A tiny minority of capitalists own not only the material means of production, but also the mental means of production— the press, TV and other instruments of propaganda. They are also bound to be supported by the capitalist state machine—the army, police and judiciary will continue to support the capitalist class.

Only when the working class holds state power can democratic rights be guaranteed.

In November 1918 the revolution in Germany got rid of the Kaiser and brought the First World War to an end. Alas, big employers like Krupps and Thyssen remained along with the generals and the reactionary army officers who set up right wing units called Freikorps. Dual power prevailed in Germany, for side by side with parliament were the workers' councils. All revolutions do not break free from the shackles of the past at one go. Side by side with the new, representing the future, the old still survives. To use Marx's words, 'The tradition of the dead generations' still hangs over the living. The events in Germany completely confirm the prophetic words of St Just, a leader of the French Revolution of 1789: 'Those who make half a revolution dig their own grave.' Under the umbrella of the Social Democratic government, Freikorps officers murdered revolutionary leaders Rosa Luxemburg and Karl Liebknecht. The revolutionary events continued with ups and downs until 1923, but they ended with the victory of capitalism. The Nazi movement was born in 1919. In 1923 it organised a 'failed' coup in Bavaria, but it was waiting in the wings. This was another lost opportunity for workers and they would pay for it dearly when Hitler came to power.

France in the 1930s saw a massive rise of working class struggle which started in February 1934 and culminated in 1936 in a decisive victory of the Popular Front—an alliance of the Communist Party, Socialist Party and Liberals (who were mistakenly called Radical Socialists—they were neither radical nor socialist). Millions of workers said to themselves, 'Now we own the government, let's take over the factories.' And in June 1936 a wave of factory occupations took place. The leaders of the Communist Party and Socialist Party, however, led a retreat following a compromise with the employers. After this the Communist Party was thrown out of the Popular Front. It was the Radical Socialist Daladier who signed the Munich agreement with Hitler in 1938, and it was the same parliament elected in the great Popular Front victory of 1936 which voted support for Marshal Pétain, head of the Vichy regime which collaborated with the Nazis from 1940 onwards.

When Indonesia won its independence from Holland in 1949 the country was led by the bourgeois nationalist Ahmed Sukarno. His ideology was based on the principles of Pancasila whose main planks were belief in god and national unity. Tragically the Indonesian Communist Party did not challenge Sukarno, but, on the contrary, agreed with him completely on the need for national unity. The result was that St Just's words came true. The Communist Party of Indonesia had far more members than the Bolshevik Party had at the time of the revolution: 3 million as against a quarter of a million. The working class of Indonesia was larger than the working class of Russia on the eve of the revolution. The peasantry was larger in Indonesia than in Russia. In 1965 a general appointed by Sukarno, one Suharto, organised a coup with the backing of the United States, the British Labour government and Australia.

Somewhere between half a million and a million people were slaughtered.

The Middle East is another area which has seen great upheavals which shook the establishment but failed to win a fundamental breakthrough. In Iraq, King Feisal was overthrown in 1951 by a mass movement. The Communist Party of Iraq was a very strong party, indeed the strongest CP in the Arab world. It entered into an alliance with the bourgeois nationalist party, the Ba'ath. The Communist Party, under Stalinist control, believed that the coming revolution would be a democratic one, which demanded an alliance between the working class and the bourgeois parties. Such an alliance means in practice the subordination of the former to the latter. The Communist Party members and the workers paid a heavy price for this alliance. The Ba'ath, headed by General Saddam Hussein, with the aid of the CIA, carried out a mass slaughter of Communists.

In Iran a general strike led to the overthrow of the Shah in 1979. *Shoras* (workers' councils) mushroomed throughout the country. Tragically the leadership of these *shoras*, largely the pro-Moscow Tudeh Party and the Fedayeen, saw the revolution as a bourgeois democratic revolution instead of a proletarian one, and so gave support to the establishment of the Islamic republic. Ayatollah Khomeini thus came to power without showing any gratitude to the Tudeh or Fedayeen, and the left was subjected to bloody repression.

I can mention a few other failed revolutions, such as Hungary 1919 and 1956, Germany 1923, China 1925-27, Spain 1936, France 1968, Portugal 1974-75.

The juxtaposition of the democratic revolution to the socialist revolution and the preference for the first is not the property of the Social Democratic leaders alone, but became the guiding line of Stalinist leaderships throughout the world.

The Russian Revolution of 1917 was an exception to the series of half-made revolutions.

The February 1917 revolution created an exciting new situation: the Tsar abdicated, centuries of the monarchy ended. The police were disbanded. In every factory workers' committees were established. In many army units soldiers committees came into being. Soviets of workers and soldiers arose everywhere.

But after the revolution in February 1917, parallel to the soviets, the old institutions continued. In the factories the old owners and the old managers continued to hold to their positions. In the army the generals were still in command: the commander-in-chief of the army was General Kornilov who was appointed by the Tsar. Parallel to soviet power was a bourgeois government headed by a liberal politician from Tsarist times. This situation, which Lenin and Trotsky called 'dual power', was full of contradictions.

Notwithstanding the nature of the soviet, its leaders begged the bourgeoisie to retain power. The majority of the soviet delegates were right wing socialists, Mensheviks and Social Revolutionaries. This was not an accident. It was the inevitable outcome of a situation in which millions of people moved to the left but still carried a lot of the ideological baggage of a Tsarist past. For millions who had hitherto supported the Tsar and the war, a move to the left did not mean straight away joining the most extreme of the parties, the Bolsheviks. The strong man of the Mensheviks, J G Tseretelli, who became minister of the interior in the bourgeois Provisional Government, explained the necessity of a compromise with the bourgeoisie: 'There can be no other road for the revolution. It's true we have all the power, and that the government would go if we lifted a finger, but that would mean disaster for the revolution.'

When, on 3 April, Lenin returned to Russia from Switzerland, he was welcomed by thousands of workers and soldiers at the Finland Station in Petrograd. Chkheidze, president of the Petrograd Soviet, welcomed him with these words: 'Comrade Lenin, in the name of the Petrograd Soviet and of the whole revolution we welcome you to Russia... But we think that the principal task of the revolutionary democracy is now the defence of the revolution from any encroachments either from within or from without. We consider that what this goal requires is not disunity, but the closing of the democratic ranks. We hope you will pursue these goals together with us.' Lenin in reply called for the continuation of the revolution as the Russian Revolution was part and parcel of the international, world revolution. The reaction of the Mensheviks to Lenin's speech was extremely hostile. Thus, I P Goldenberg, a former member of the Bolshevik Central Committee, declared, 'Lenin has now made himself a candidate for one European throne that has been vacant for 30 years—the throne of Bakunin! Lenin's new words echo something old—the superannuated truths of primitive anarchism.'

Lenin did not adapt himself to the Mensheviks and Social Revolutionaries, who were the embodiment of petty-bourgeois democracy. He followed consistently the call of Marx at the time of the 1848 revolution in France and Germany, to be completely independent of the petty-bourgeois democratic camp. Marx wrote, 'The German workers...must contribute most to their final victory, by informing themselves of their own class interests, by taking up their independent political position as soon as possible, by not allowing themselves to be misled by the hypocritical phrases of the democratic petty bourgeoisie into doubting for one minute the necessity of an independently organised party of the proletariat. Their battle cry must be: 'The permanent revolution.'

After days, weeks and months of stormy events the Bolsheviks managed to win over the majority of workers. On 9 September the Petrograd soviet went over to Bolshevism and Trotsky was elected as its president. On the same day the Bolsheviks won the majority of the Moscow soviet. From this point it was only a small stride towards the attainment of workers' power on 7 November 1917.

The working class, not the party, makes the revolution, but the party guides the working class. As Trotsky aptly wrote, 'Without a guiding organisation the energy of the masses would dissipate like steam not endorsed in a piston box. But nevertheless what moves things is not the piston or the box, but the steam.'

The difference between success and failure, between Russia in October 1917 and the other workers' revolutions, was that in the former case there was a mass revolutionary party providing effective leadership. While socialists cannot determine the moment when the revolutionary crisis breaks, they do determine the eventual outcome by the degree to which they build a strong revolutionary party.

Cato the Elder, a member of the Roman Senate, used to end all his speeches with the following words: 'Cartago delenda est'—Carthage must be destroyed. And, finally, Rome did destroy Carthage. We have to end with the words, 'The revolutionary party must be built.'

Chapter 13

Marxism and democracy

Turkish socialists, friends of mine, tell me that there is a widespread belief in Turkey that if the country joins the European Community, democracy will be guaranteed. Before dealing with this specific argument, I would like to develop a more general picture about the relations between democracy and a change in society.

The word 'democracy' was coined in ancient Athens, and it means 'rule of the people'. However, neither slaves, nor women, nor non-Athenian residents, were entitled to vote in this democracy,

Universal suffrage by itself does not guarantee rule by the people. As a matter of fact it was Napoleon III who used universal suffrage to impose his dictatorship through plebiscites: the central state mobilised the backward provinces against advanced Paris. Similarly Bismarck, who introduced universal suffrage to Germany, used it to strengthen the power of the Kaiser, the princes and the Junkers against the socialists of Berlin.

When one looks at democratic capitalist states like Britain, France or Germany, one finds that there is universal suffrage, members of parliament are elected democratically, but the democracy is formalistic and skin-deep. Members of parliament are elected, but the judges, police officers and army commanders are not. Above all, people have no right to democratically elect the boss of the factory, nor to remove him if they wish. Capitalists and proletarians are equal in the eyes of the law. When the law says, 'Neither the poor nor the rich are allowed to sleep in the park,' formally they are equal. In the same way, when the law says, 'Everyone, rich and poor, is entitled to stay at the Ritz Hotel,' the law does not discriminate against the poor.

The paper magnate in Britain has only one vote, like any other citizen. As a matter of fact, Rupert Murdoch, who controls a massive press empire—his daily paper the *Sun* sells four million copies a day; in addition he has the *Times*, the *News of the World* with a massive circulation, and the *Sunday Times*—has no vote, being a US citizen, which he took up for commercial reasons. British workers pay 23 percent of their wages in income tax and 10 percent in national insurance.

Rupert Murdoch pays only 0.5 percent of his profits in tax, as he registers his companies in the Cayman Islands tax haven. Of course the workers and the capitalists are equal in the eyes of the law. Of course the printer who works for Murdoch is not disadvantaged legally. I am ready to bet that if I went in for the Olympics to race against Linford Christie, the quickest sprinter in Britain, I would beat him, although I am 82 years old, on condition that I sit in a good car with a good chauffeur.

Above all, formal democracy does not eliminate the oppression of nations or races. In Rhodesia (now Zimbabwe), the 200,000 white inhabitants had democratic rights. This did not undermine the oppression of the five million blacks. On the contrary, it strengthened the unity of the whites against the blacks.

The fact that Israel is a democratic state does not mean that the three million Palestinians, thrown out of their land by this same state, have the right to return to their land, or the right to determine their destiny. The key criterion whether popular democracy is being strengthened, is the extent to which the oppressed gain real power. In 1902 Lenin wrote that when a worker goes on strike for wages, he is simply a trade unionist. But when he goes on strike against the beating of Jews, then he is a real revolutionary socialist. He went on to say, 'We are the tribune of the oppressed.' In a state in which there is a dominant nation and an oppressed nation, a central duty of socialists belonging to the dominant nation, is to fight for the right of self determination of the oppressed. To get unity between the proletariat of the oppressed nation and the oppressor nation, it is necessary for the proletariat of the oppressor nation to put the emphasis on the right of separation of the oppressed; while the proletariat of the oppressed nation has to argue strongly for unity with the proletariat of the oppressor nation.

The precondition for the above is that the oppression of a nation damages not only the proletariat of the oppressed nation, but also of the ruling nation. A white worker in the United States is privileged vis-á-vis a black worker. This is much more visible in, let us say Texas, than in New York, where wages, jobs, housing for white workers are better than for black people in Texas. And therefore, on the face of it, of course the white workers benefit from the oppression of blacks. But wages and labour conditions and houses of white workers in Texas are much worse than in New York.

The key for real active, popular democracy is the struggle of workers united across race, nationality and gender.

When I watched the television and saw the terrible impact of the earthquake on northwest Turkey last year, it was so obvious that the earthquake did terrible damage to slum houses, whether inhabited by Turks or Kurds, while the houses of the wealthy were not affected. The pictures also showed clearly the role of the army. The Turkish army is the second biggest army in NATO, surpassed only by that of the United States. When it came to the earthquake you could see soldiers coming quickly to keep order, with guns, not bulldozers to save lives.

Turkey joining the European Common Market will in no way raise the self-activity of workers. The key for Marxists is the self activity of the mass of the workers. Of course every democratic right, however small, has to be treasured. But real mass democracy cannot be achieved except by mass action. As Marx put it, 'The emancipation of the working class is the act of the working class.'

The whole tradition of the education system is that history is made from above. We learn about history and kings, emperors and generals. And therefore the illusion that if the prime minister of Turkey sits together with Tony Blair, Gerhard Schröder and Jospin, it raises real democracy, is an illusion we have to abolish,

Workers cannot achieve power by tricks, behind the back of history, but only by the class struggle.

Chapter 14

Is world revolution possible?

The industrial working class in South Korea today is larger than the world working class at the time Marx died in 1883. Workers at present are more numerous than peasants. The social and political weight of the working class is incomparably larger than that of the mass of peasants. Workers work in big units of production. Sometimes tens of thousands of them are employed by the same corporation, while the peasantry is atomised, fragmented. Every peasant family works on its own on a little plot of land.

Marx argued that a revolution becomes necessary when the productive forces come into conflict with the old relations of production, the old economic structure.

The capitalists at the dawn of their system were not only progressive, but revolutionary, as they fought against the fetters of feudalism. The English bourgeoisie made a revolution in the 17th century, establishing its economic, social and political supremacy. The same was done in the 18th century by the French bourgeoisie. A few years after the French revolution the capitalists in Britain's American colonies declared their independence and established supreme power. The United States was born.

It is obvious that today capitalist relations of production are an impediment to the development of the productive forces. The fact that hundreds of thousands, if not millions, of building workers are unemployed, while hundreds of millions lack decent housing, demonstrates this. Millions of people are starving, not because there is not enough food around, but because they can't afford to buy the food. One anecdote, told to me years ago, illustrates the situation. A child says to his father in the midst of winter, 'It is so cold. Why don't you make a fire?' The father answers, 'I can't afford to buy coal. I have no money.' The child: 'Why haven't you any money'. 'Because I am unemployed'. 'Why are you unemployed'? 'Silly boy, don't you know? I used to be a miner, and there is too much coal in the world.'

The victory of the bourgeoisie over the feudal lords was absolutely inevitable. They coexisted. The capitalists could turn to the feudal lord and say, 'We are richer than you, and our wealth increases all the time, while your wealth is dwindling. The best proof of our superiority is the fact that quite often, when members of the nobility find themselves in economic difficulties, they try to marry my daughters, to mix gold with their blue blood. Intellectually we are far superior to you. You have the Bible; we have the Encyclopedia. You have the Church, we have the universities. You have the priests; we have professors. We influence far more members of your class than you influence members of our class.' This was demonstrated clearly on the eve of the French Revolution, when the États généraux met. This body was divided into three Estates: the top one was the nobility, the second the priesthood, the third the capitalists—the middle class. When it came to voting, members of the first two estates broke ranks and joined the Third Estate.

The working class relation to the capitalists is fundamentally different from that of the capitalists to the feudal lords. The worker cannot come to the capitalist and say: 'You own the factories, the banks, the shipyards, while we own... When you are in financial trouble, you don't rush to find a worker to marry your daughter.' While the *Sun* sells four million copies a day, mainly to working people, I doubt if there are any capitalists who buy socialist papers. Because of that, it is not inevitable that workers will win in every revolution. As Marx said, 'The prevailing ideas in every society are the ideas of the ruling class.' He also wrote that communists generalise the international and historical experience of the working class. Nobody has personal experience of those events, No one alive today was active in the Paris Commune, in the Russian Revolution of 1905, 1917, etc. The revolutionary party is the memory of the class; it is the university of the working class. Therefore there is no inevitability that workers will be victorious in every revolution.

On the question, is world revolution possible? The answer is, not only is it possible, but it is inevitable. The world capitalist system is like a chain composed of a number of links of national states. When the pressure reaches extremes, one of the links is bound to break. When this happens it affects other links. The Russian Revolution of 1917 was the beginning of a world revolution. It was followed by the German Revolution of 1918, by the revolution in the Austro-Hungarian Empire in 1919, by the mass occupations of factories in Italy in 1920-21, by the continuation of the German Revolution culminating at the end of

1923. The Communist parties mushroomed. In 1916, at the International conference in Zimmerwald of socialists opposing the war, Rosa Luxemburg made the ironic comment, 'We have reached a situation that the whole international anti-war movement can travel in a few carriages pulled by horses.' In 1920 the Communist Party of Germany had half a million members, the French 200,000 the Italian a similar number.

To say that the world revolution is inevitable does not mean that it is bound to be victorious.

The 1930s in slow motion

Some ten years ago I argued that we are entering a period that is like a film of the 1930s in slow motion. We sank into a world recession, but much shallower than the one of 1929-33. At that time in Germany there were 8 million unemployed, and no unemployment benefit. Today there are 4 million unemployed with unemployment benefit that is above the average wage in Britain. It is true that Le Pen imitates Hitler, but his support is incomparably softer than Hitler's. Besides the 13 million votes Hitler won in 1933, he had tens of thousands of armed Nazis, Stormtroops, aimed at smashing workers' organisation. The National Front in France has nothing like that. Its support is much softer. When the mass strikes took place in France in November-December 1995 it shattered the support of the National Front. With the collapse of its support the National Front split, and Le Pen remained with a rump of the organisation.

Again, it would be a mistake to look at the 1930s simply as days of darkness, and that is all. The defeat of the German working class by Hitler was a catastrophe that cannot be overestimated. But at the same time we had the mass occupation of factories in France in June 1936 that raised the spectre of revolution. Alas, the leadership of the strike, the Communist Party and Socialist Party, joined forces with the Liberals to contain the struggle. This coalition, under the name Popular Front, three years later voted to support Marshal Pétain's collaboration with the Nazis.

The 1930s were a decade of extremes. Anyone sitting on the fence was only helping the reactionary forces. The fact that the film of the 1930s returns, but in slow motion, means there is much greater opportunity to stop the film and direct it in the way we want. The key is building the revolutionary party. As Trotsky wrote, the mass struggle is like steam, and the revolutionary party is the piston that directs the machine. A piston without steam is a dead piece of metal; steam without a piston is diffuse and leads you nowhere.

Coming back to the title of this article, we can sum up our answer with the following words: world revolution is not only possible, but inevitable, but its victory is not inevitable.

PS: Rereading this article, I became aware that it is possible the reader might take Marxism to be a dogmatic collection of iron laws of history. As a matter of fact Marx always knew that accidents play a significant role in history. Had Lenin died just before returning to Russia in 1917 the impact on the Bolshevik Party would have been massive and hence on the history of the revolution.

Other accidents can accelerate historical development. I shall give one example. The earthquake in north west Turkey last year led to the collapse of slum houses where Turkish workers live, and also Kurdish workers who were recent refugees from south east Turkey. At the same time the well-built houses of the rich hardly suffered from the earthquake. This accident could have been used by revolutionary socialists to argue that class is the main divide in society, that Turkish and Kurdish workers are brothers.

Chapter 15

The millennium: between hope and fear

The *Communist Manifesto* written by Karl Marx and Friedrich Engels in 1848 states:

> The history of all hitherto existing society is the history of class struggles. Freeman and slave, patrician and plebeian, lord and serf, guildmaster and journeyman, in a word, oppressor and oppressed, stood in constant opposition to one another, carried on an uninterrupted, now hidden, now open fight, a fight that each time ended, either in a revolutionary reconstitution of society at large, or in the common ruin of the contending classes.

The slave rebellion, led by Spartacus, and all other slave rebellions, were defeated. This did not lead to a continuation of the slave system in the Roman Empire. The slaves were replaced by colons (serfs). Feudalism replaced slavery. This process was accelerated by the invasion of the German tribes into the Roman Empire.

Again, when we speak about the transition from feudalism to capitalism, quite often it sounds like a very smooth process. One can spend half an hour reading a chapter on feudalism, and then move on to a chapter on capitalism. But the process was much less smooth, much more contradictory. Feudalism survived for over a millennium in Europe. When it was in decline and capitalism was rising in the cracks of feudal society, it was not a one-way street leading upwards. As a matter of fact, Arab Spain in the 11th century was much more advanced than Spain three centuries later. In the 17th century, during the Thirty Years War (1618-48), the population of Germany was cut by nearly a half.

Again, the horrors of feudalism went on unabated. To give one example: for 1,000 years the lord of the manor had the right to deflower any young maid in the villages under his control. The oppression of the serfs, above all their female section, continued for a very long time.

Capitalism is far more dynamic than any previous system of economy and society. Hence the extremes appear on a far more dramatic scale than ever before. Capitalism developed the productive forces to a massive extent, so that plenty for all is possible. At the same time capitalism is torn by competition between different capitalists and different capitalist states. The competition between General Motors and Ford forced them to increase the exploitation of both their workforces. The anarchic competition between the capitalists imposes tyranny over the workers in every capitalist enterprise. Extreme wealth coexists with dreadful poverty. Famines are not new phenomena for humanity; we have had them for thousands of years. But they were the result of the scarcity of food. Today, under capitalism, we have millions starving while there is surplus grain in the world. The extremities can be shown by one simple example. It is estimated that 20 million children die every year for lack of clean water. The profit of Bill Gates, the richest man in the world, in one year, would be enough to create water pipes and dig wells that guarantee that no child be deprived of clean water. One year's profit!

Competition between the capitalists, of course, takes not only economic forms, but also military forms.

With the outbreak of the First World War, Rosa Luxemburg, the great Polish-German revolutionary, wrote that the alternatives before humanity were 'socialism or barbarism'.

We know far more about barbarism than she could know. She was murdered in January 1919, before the gas chambers, before the atomic bombs falling on Hiroshima and Nagasaki were invented.

At the beginning of the 1990s I stated that observing the 1990s in Europe was like watching a film of the 1930s in slow motion.

In the last 20 years the world has gone through three world recessions. But they were pale imitations of the dreadful crash of 1929-33. It is true, an extreme right wing movement—fascism—rose in Europe. But Le Pen is only a pale imitation of Hitler. It is true that the National Front of Le Pen did get the support of 5 million voters as against Hitler's 13 million. But the difference in the quality of support for the two was radical. Hitler's support was frenzied petty bourgeois who lost everything in the crash. Le Pen's mass support was not as angry. Hitler had armed Stormtroops even before he came to office in January 1933. Le Pen's supporters were involved here and there in physical attacks on immigrants.

The other side of the coin—workers' struggles—are also a pale imitation of the 1930s. It is true that the level of industrial struggle in France rose during the 1990s. But even the mass strikes of November-December 1995 cannot be compared with the mass occupation of factories in France in June 1936.

The fact that the story of the 1990s is like a film of the 1930s in slow motion means, first of all, that it is much more open to stop the film than if it was speedy.

Even more significant is the political situation in the working class, that is far more favourable for revolutionaries than it was in the 1930s. In the 1930s Stalinist parties dominated the left throughout the whole of Europe. Of course the victory of Hitler was not inevitable. Trotsky argued brilliantly for the need for a united front of the Communist and Social Democratic parties in Germany to stop Hitler. Hitler could have been stopped. First of all, the vote for the Social Democratic Party of 8 million and the Communist Party of 6 million was larger than the vote for the Nazis. Even more significant was the quality of the support for the workers' parties. Trotsky wrote of the Nazi support as being 'human dust'—isolated individuals—while the workers' parties had massive power, in the factories, on the railways, etc. Hitler was not stopped because the Stalinist policy was against the united front; Stalin characterised the Social Democrats as 'social fascists'.

Again, the occupation of the factories in France in 1936 could have been the springboard for proletarian revolution, not only in France, but in kindling the revolution elsewhere, eg in Germany. Alas, the Stalinists argued for coalition with the liberal party, all in the interests of the foreign policy of Stalin. The result was that in 1940 the parliament that was elected in May 1936 under the banner of the Popular Front voted its support for Marshal Pétain, head of the French government, now co-operating with Nazi Germany.

Today the power of the Stalinist parties in Europe has collapsed following the disintegration of the state capitalist regimes in Russia and Eastern Europe. Now there is a very wide space for revolutionaries to build.

The millennium both gives us hope and alerts us to the dangers. We live in an epoch of extremes, of extreme possibilities and extreme dangers. We should follow the wise advice of the philosopher Spinoza, who wrote, 'One should not laugh, neither cry, but understand.' We live in a period of extreme possibilities.

The *Communist Manifesto* described the working class as the gravediggers of capitalism. At present the international working class is incomparably stronger than at the time the *Manifesto* was written. The number of industrial workers in South Korea alone is larger than the total industrial working class of the world when Marx died in 1883. We have a world to win.

The Battle of Seattle demonstrated massive anger against the capitalist corporations. The German mass circulation paper *Der Spiegel*, commenting about the demonstration in Seattle, said that it shows that the next millennium will begin with a war against capitalism. For many years the word anti-capitalism was part of the vocabulary of small revolutionary organisations. Now it is part of the language of millions.